WIZARD BOOKS

CURSE OF THE MUMMY

Jerran Farr, renowned archaeologist, is looking for a hired help for an expedition to the Desert of Skulls, where he plans to excavate the tomb of an ancient pharaoh. It seems a nice, easy and, above all, safe task for an adventurer like YOU. But when that tomb turns out to belong to Akharis, legendary ruler from a previous age, and when a crazed cult of his followers is trying to return the evil pharaoh to life, matters are guaranteed to turn deadly serious. Soon you will learn the true meaning of the Curse of the Mummy! It will take a real hero to defeat Akharis and win the treasure from the tomb. Are YOU that hero?

Two dice, a pencil and an eraser are all you need to embark on this deadly adventure which comes complete with its own combat system and a score sheet to record your progress. Innumerable dangers lie ahead and your success is anything but certain. It's up to YOU to decide which route to follow, which dangers to risk and which foes to fight! Can YOU defeat the Curse of Akharis?

The Fighting Fantasy Gamebooks

STEVE JACKSON AND IAN LIVINGSTONE

CURSE OF THE MUMMY

BY JONATHAN GREEN
ILLUSTRATED BY MARTIN McKENNA

Wizard Books

This edition published in the UK in 2007 by Wizard Books,
an imprint of Icon Books Ltd., The Old Dairy,
Brook Road, Thriplow, Cambridge SG8 7RG
email: wizard@iconbooks.co.uk
www.iconbooks.co.uk/wizard

First published by the Penguin Group in 1995

Sold in the UK, Europe, South Africa and Asia by
Faber and Faber Ltd., 3 Queen Square, London WC1N 3AU
or their agents

Distributed in the UK, Europe, South Africa and Asia by
TBS Ltd., Frating Distribution Centre, Colchester Road,
Frating Green, Colchester CO7 7DW

Published in Australia in 2007 by Allen & Unwin Pty. Ltd.,
PO Box 8500, 83 Alexander Street, Crows Nest, NSW 2065

Distributed in Canada by Penguin Books Canada,
90 Eglinton Avenue East, Suite 700, Toronto, Ontario M4P 2Y3

ISBN-10: 1-84046-802-5
ISBN-13: 978-1840468-02-1

Printed and bound in the UK by Cox & Wyman Ltd., Reading

CONTENTS

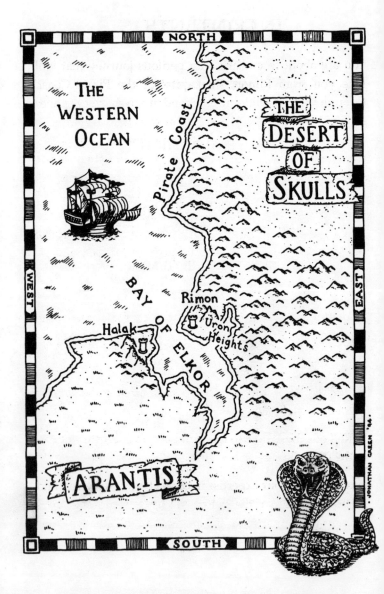

INTRODUCTION

You are about to embark on a perilous journey that will take you from Rimon, the capital of the Pirate Coast, through the arid wilderness beyond, up to the very fringes of the Desert of Skulls itself. Before you launch into your adventure, you must first determine your strengths and weaknesses. You use dice to work out your initial scores. On pages 16–17 is an *Adventure Sheet*, which you may use to record the details of your adventure. On it you will find boxes for recording your SKILL, STAMINA and LUCK scores. You are advised either to mark them in pencil or make photocopies of the blank sheet for use in future adventures.

Skill, Stamina and Luck

To determine your *Initial* SKILL, STAMINA and LUCK scores:

- Roll one die. Add 6 to this number and enter this total in the SKILL box on the *Adventure Sheet*.

- Roll two dice. Add 12 to the number rolled and enter this total in the STAMINA box.

- Roll one die. Add 6 to this number and enter this total in the LUCK box.

SKILL reflects your expertise in combat, your dexterity and agility; the higher the better. STAMINA represents your strength; the higher it is, the longer you will survive. Your LUCK score indicates how lucky a person you are.

SKILL, STAMINA and LUCK scores change constantly during an adventure, so keep an eraser handy. You must keep an accurate record of these scores, but never rub out your *Initial* scores. Although you may receive additional SKILL, STAMINA and LUCK points, their totals may never exceed your *Initial* scores, except on very rare occasions when the text specifically tells you so.

Battles

During your adventure you will often encounter hostile creatures which will attack you, and you yourself may choose to draw your sword against an enemy you chance across. In some situations you may be given special options, allowing you to deal with the encounter in an unusual manner, but in most cases you will have to resolve battles as described below.

Enter your opponent's SKILL and STAMINA scores in the first empty *Encounter Box* on your *Adventure Sheet*. You should also make a note of any special abilities or instructions which are unique to that particular opponent. Then follow this sequence:

1. Roll two dice for your opponent. Add its SKILL score to the total rolled. This total is **its** Attack Strength.

2. Roll two dice for yourself, then add your current SKILL score. This total is **your** Attack Strength.

3. If your Attack Strength is higher than your opponent's, you have wounded it: proceed to step 4. If the opponent's Attack Strength is higher than yours, it has wounded you: proceed to step 5. If both Attack Strength totals are the same, you have avoided or parried each other's blows – start a new Attack Round from step 1, above.

4. You have wounded your opponent, so subtract 2 points from **its** STAMINA score. You may use LUCK here to do additional damage (see 'Using Luck in Battles' below). Proceed to step 6.

5. Your opponent has wounded you, so subtract 2 points from **your** STAMINA score. You may use LUCK to minimize the damage (see 'Using Luck in Battles' below). Proceed to step 6.

6. Begin the next Attack Round, starting again at step 1. This sequence continues until the STAMINA score of either you or your opponent reaches zero, which means death. If your opponent dies you are free to continue with your adventure. If you die you must start all over again by creating a new character.

Fighting More Than One Opponent

Sometimes you will find yourself under attack from more than one person or creature in combat. Sometimes you will treat them as a single opponent; sometimes you will be able to fight each in turn; at other times you will have to fight them all at once! If they are treated as a single opponent, the combat is resolved normally. When you are instructed to fight your opponents one at a time, the combat is again resolved normally – except that when you defeat an enemy the next one steps forward to fight you! If you find yourself under attack from more than one opponent at the same time, each adversary will make a separate attack on you in the course of each Attack Round, but you can choose which one to fight. Attack your chosen target as in normal battle. Against any additional opponents you roll the dice for your Attack Strength in the normal way; if your Attack Strength is greater than your opponent's, you will not inflict a wound. Just regard this as though you have parried an incoming blow. However, if your Attack Strength is lower than your opponent's you will have been wounded in the normal way. Of course, you will have to settle the outcome of each additional adversary separately.

Luck

In certain paragraphs you will be told to *Test your Luck*, and you will then find out the consequences of being Lucky or Unlucky. At various times during your adventure you may use LUCK to make an outcome more favourable to you. But beware! Using LUCK is a risky business and, if you are Unlucky, the results could be disastrous.

The way you *Test your Luck* is as follows:

Roll two dice. If the number rolled is *less than* or *equal to* your current LUCK score, you have been Lucky. If the number rolled is *higher* than your current LUCK score, you have been Unlucky and will be penalised.

Each time you *Test your Luck*, you must subtract one point from your current LUCK score. So the more you rely on LUCK, the more risky this procedure becomes.

Using Luck in Battles

In battles, you always have the option of using your LUCK, either to inflict a more serious wound on an opponent or to minimize the effects of a wound you have just received.

If you have just wounded an opponent: you may *Test your Luck* as described above. If you are Lucky, subtract an extra 2 points from your opponent's STAMINA score (i.e. 4 instead of 2 normally). But if you are Unlucky, your blow only scratches your opponent and you deduct only 1 point from your opponent's STAMINA (instead of scoring the normal 2 points of damage, you now score only 1).

If the opponent has just wounded you: you can *Test your Luck* to try to minimize the wound. If you are Lucky, your opponent's blow only grazes you; deduct only 1 point from your STAMINA. If you are Unlucky, your wound is serious and you must deduct 1 extra STAMINA point (i.e. a total of 3 points from your own STAMINA).

Remember: you must subtract 1 point from your LUCK score each time you *Test your Luck*.

More About Your Attributes

Skill

Your SKILL score will not change much during the course of your adventure. Occasionally a paragraph may give instructions to increase or decrease your SKILL score, but it may not exceed its *Initial* value unless you are specifically instructed to the contrary.

At various times during your adventure you will be told to *Test your Skill*. The procedure for this is exactly the same as that for *Testing your Luck*: roll two dice. If the number rolled is less than or equal to your current score, you have succeeded in your test and the result will go in your favour. If the number rolled is higher than your current SKILL score, you have failed the test and will have to suffer the consequences. However, unlike *Testing your Luck*, do not subtract 1 point from your SKILL each time you *Test your Skill*.

Stamina and Provisions

Your STAMINA score will change a lot during the adventure. It will drop as a result of wounds received through combat, or by falling foul of traps and pitfalls; and it will also drop after you perform any particularly arduous task. If your STAMINA score ever falls to zero or below, you have been killed and should stop reading the book immediately. Brave adventurers who wish to pursue their quest must roll up a new character and start all over again.

You can restore lost STAMINA by eating meals or Provisions. You start the game without any Provisions, but during your adventure you will be able to obtain meals. You must keep track of how many meals' worth of Provisions you have remaining by filling in the details in the Provisions box on your *Adventure Sheet*. Each time you eat a meal you may restore up to 4 points of STAMINA, but remember to deduct 1 meal from your Provisions box. You may rest and eat Provisions at any time except when engaged in battle.

Luck

Additions to your LUCK score may be awarded in the adventure when you have been particularly Lucky or created your own Luck by some action. Details are given, where appropriate, in the paragraphs of the book. Remember that, as with SKILL and STAMINA, your LUCK score may not exceed its *Initial* value unless specifically instructed on a page.

Poison

You have spent many years adventuring in the dangerous lands of southern Allansia. As a result, you have been exposed to various poisons on many occasions and, in defence, your body has built up some immunity to their effects. Throughout your latest adventure you will no doubt be exposed to the bites and stings of venomous creatures, or you will encounter enemies who have no qualms about using poisoned weapons against you. Although you can recover STAMINA lost to the effects of poison (as explained above), the build-up of toxins in your body may still prove fatal. Whenever you are told to increase your POISON score, record it carefully on your *Adventure Sheet*. You begin your adventure with a poison score of zero. Should your POISON total ever equal or exceed 18, the toxins coursing through your bloodstream will kill you and your adventure will end there and then. The only way to reduce your POISON score is by the use of certain potions and charms, or in certain exceptional circumstances.

Equipment

You have begun your adventure with very little equipment indeed: just a sword, a backpack to hold your Provisions and treasure, and 5 Gold Pieces. To begin with, you do not have a lantern or any Provisions. Note down the Gold Pieces in the appropriate box on your *Adventure Sheet*; everything else goes in the Equipment box, as will any other useful items you may find or purchase on your travels.

Alternative Dice

If you do not have a pair of dice handy, dice rolls are printed throughout the book at the bottom of the pages. Flicking rapidly throughout the book and stopping on a page will give you a random dice roll. If you need to 'roll' only one die, read only the first printed die; if two, total the two dice symbols.

ADVENTURE SHEET

SKILL	STAMINA	LUCK
Initial Skill = 7	*Initial* Stamina = 21 19	*Initial* Luck = 7

POISON	PROVISIONS	GOLD PIECES
		53 36 33 26

EQUIPMENT AND TREASURE

Sword Oil + lantern
Alabaster scarabab

NOTES

MONSTER ENCOUNTER BOXES

Skill = *Stamina =*	*Skill =* *Stamina =*	*Skill =* *Stamina =*
Skill = *Stamina =*	*Skill =* *Stamina =*	*Skill =* *Stamina =*
Skill = *Stamina =*	*Skill =* *Stamina =*	*Skill =* *Stamina =*
Skill = *Stamina =*	*Skill =* *Stamina =*	*Skill =* *Stamina =*

BACKGROUND

Facing its twin, Halak, on the other side of the mouth of the Bay of Elkor, Rimon is the capital of the Pirate Coast. With their ramshackle mazes of streets and twisting alley-ways, the two ancient towns, perched on the steeply sloping sides of twin mountain peaks, are a haven for buccaneers and renegades: even the feared pirate captain Garius of Halak has his secret hideout somewhere along the coast. It was a crew of these scurvy pirates who attacked the merchantman on which you had gained passage, travelling north from Kaynlesh-Ma and making for Port Blacksand. Your vessel was sunk and all on board were left to the mercy of the sea.

After several days you were washed ashore – as far as you know, the only survivor of the wreck – with only your sword and enough money to keep you from starvation for just a few days. Finding yourself not far from Rimon, you made your way to the town, hoping to find work guarding a caravan heading north, but you missed the last one to leave for several weeks by only a day. So instead you decided to find gainful employment that might earn you your passage on another ship heading for Port Blacksand.

Then you saw a notice nailed to a wall in the Adventurer's Guild. The notice read: 'Brave warrior required for dangerous mission into hills around the Desert of

Skulls. Great rewards guaranteed. Apply Jerran Farr, The Monkey's Paw'. You made some discreet enquiries about this possible employer and discovered that he is an archaeologist of some notoriety; he does not enjoy a very good reputation among the adventuring fraternity of Rimon and is considered by most to be no better than a tomb-robber. However, times are hard, so you decided you had nothing to lose and made your way to the Monkey's Paw, a seedy drinking-house in one of the poorer parts of Rimon.

Entering the bar, you find the clientele as shady-looking as you would expect, and the landlord looks as if he would cut your throat as soon as serve you a drink. You mention Jerran Farr's name, and with a grunt the landlord directs you to a man sitting at a table by himself. Jerran Farr, a moustached man in his mid-thirties, looks as if he too has known his fair share of hardship; he is tanned from days of toil in the baking lands at the edge of the Desert of Skulls and his sleeveless leather jacket, like the rest of his clothes, is worn and dusty and he wears a battered wide-brimmed hat to keep off the sun. Having made your introductions, you sit down opposite the man.

'Have you heard of the Curse of Akharis?' Jerran asks. You shake your head. 'Then I will tell you of the legend. Centuries ago, before the drowning of Atlantis by the gods, the three major continents of Titan — Allansia, the Old World and Khul — were all joined together as one massive continent which early records call Irritaria. At this time, at the southern edge of what we now know as the Desert of Skulls, there existed a small desert kingdom called Djarat. The people of Djarat, who worshipped a whole clutch of animal-headed gods, carried out the practice of mummifying their dead rulers before burying them in great tombs in the mountains, along with fabulous riches. Akharis was the last of the rulers of Djarat to be buried before the parting of the lands. He favoured Sithera, the Goddess of Evil, above all the other gods of Djarat and was the cruellest tyrant the kingdom had ever known. He demanded human sacrifices for his goddess and was said to commune with dark spirits and bring the mummies of his ancestors back to life. When at last he died, poisoned by one of his enemies, he was aged one hundred and fifty-six. As he lay, dying, Akharis called on Sithera, saying that one day he would return and all would suffer under his curse: plagues of flies, snakes and scorpions would come upon the land, the daytime sky would be as black as at night, and the cities would be swallowed by the desert. Legend says he was buried, surrounded by piles of priceless treasures, in one of the most astonishing tombs ever constructed, one which included many terrible death-traps.'

'Interesting as all this is, what does it have to do with you wanting to hire a brave warrior for a dangerous mission?' you ask the archaeologist.

'Let me explain,' Jerran continues. 'Five days ago I was working at a site on the edge of the rocky hills bordering Rimon when a man staggered into my camp. He was terribly dehydrated, suffering from sun-stroke, and he looked as if he had been in a battle. I gave him water and tried to make him as comfortable as possible. As soon as he had recovered a little, he told me what had happened to him. He was part of a group of explorers who had been investigating the lands at the edge of the desert. He told me that at a ruined temple by an oasis they uncovered an inscription that revealed the location of the lost tomb of Akharis with all its treasures. They set out to find it at once, but they had not gone very far when they were ambushed by a group of people, swathed in red robes that bore the emblem of a golden cobra. The rest of his party were either captured or killed and he was left for dead. When it was safe, he started the difficult journey back to Rimon to warn the people what was happening, but he only made it as far as my camp. He died the next morning.'

Absorbed by Jerran's tale, you ask, 'So who were these red-robed attackers?'

'Members of the Cult of the Cobra,' he replies. 'This cult was the priesthood that worshipped Sithera in Djarat and they were Akharis's most loyal followers. It has always been their aim to find Akharis's tomb and resurrect their long-dead master, so that he could call down his curse upon the land and reclaim his kingdom. The secret sect has been revived in the last decade and it looks as if the Cult of the Cobra have at last found his tomb and are preparing for their king's return. They must be stopped, or all will suffer the Curse of Akharis. I need one brave warrior to accompany me and infiltrate the cult without their knowing, to thwart their evil plans. If you will help me — and should we succeed – the treasures of the tomb will be our reward.'

'Of course I will help you carry out your plan,' you say. The possible riches to be found in the tomb could make you wealthy beyond your wildest dreams – but, more important than that, the cult must be stopped from bringing such an evil back into the world. There is no time to lose. You both leave the Monkey's Paw immediately to prepare for your quest.

The pair of you have not gone far along a narrow back street on your way towards the markets of Rimon when a figure, covered from head to toe in fine red robes, drops silently from the top of a wall to the ground in front of you, and a harsh, hissing voice behind you says, 'Not so fast, Jerran Farr.'

Turn to paragraph 1.

1

You spin around, to see two more people dressed in the same manner as the first, only their eyes visible between the swathes of red cloth. Their robes bear the emblem of a rearing golden cobra: they must be members of Akharis's evil cult. Each of the cultists is armed with a long curving sword, and an assortment of other silent death-weapons hangs from their belts. 'They must have discovered that the explorer survived their attack and they followed his trail to my camp,' Jerran whispers under his breath, 'and from there they must have followed me to Rimon. What shall we do?'

Will you:

Draw your sword and run at the cultists' leader?	Turn to **185**
Draw your sword and stand your ground?	Turn to **68**
Try to escape?	Turn to **259**

2

As you run for the exit from the inner sanctum of the Temple of Sithera, the roof gives way and you are crushed under tonnes of rubble. Your adventure ends here.

3

The treasure snake slumps to the ground, leaving it safe for you to search its chamber. In fact there is no gold or gems here — it was all the Scitalis's illusion. However, in one corner of the room is a small earthenware pot, decorated all over with hieroglyphs. When you

translate them with your papyrus scroll, they turn out
to be prayers asking for everlasting life. Taking the lid
off the jar, all you find inside is a bundle of preserving
bandages. You are not sure what it is or what purpose
it serves, but if you want to take the earthenware jar
add it to your *Adventure Sheet*. Leaving the Scitalis's
room, will you head along the adjoining passage you
passed earlier, if you have not already done so (turn to
370), or retrace your steps past the Decayer's room
and follow the new branch (turn to **63**)?

4

Suddenly you see that the river ahead disappears
under a rock-face in front of you. You have no choice
but to hold your breath and hope for the best . . .

You come to the surface, gasping for air, and are
surprised to find yourself in a flooded room. *Test your
Luck*, adding 2 to the dice roll. If you are Unlucky,
your provisions have all been ruined by your river
journey (remove them all from your *Adventure Sheet*).
You are able to wade towards an archway that leads
out of the chamber, only waist-deep in the water.
Beyond it, you find yourself in an expanse of flooded

corridors and passageways and begin to explore them. Coming to an intersection, you have to choose your route ahead. Will you go to the left (turn to **48**), to the right (turn to **195**), or straight on (turn to **124**)?

5

You have not travelled many kilometres before you reach the top of a ridge of a line of hills and find yourself looking out over a wide valley. The land drops steeply down to the sand-covered valley floor and there, only a few hundred metres away, lie the fallen pillars and broken walls of a temple, half buried by the desert. At last you have found it! In front of the temple is a sparkling oasis, surrounded by palm trees, its clear waters looking very inviting after your days of hot and dusty travel. Here, you hope, you will discover the location of Akharis's tomb. Where will you make for first: for the oasis (turn to **164**) or the ruins (turn to **346**)?

6

With a rumbling groan the stone door swings open. Your light illuminates a small, square chamber which is empty, except for a low stone altar in front of a life-size carving of a ram-headed man. Full of curiosity, you enter, when a voice suddenly speaks to you in a language you do not understand. 'Then I grant you the Wisdom of Khunam,' the voice concludes. Just like the rest of the speech, that last sentence was not spoken in Allansian, but it was comprehensible! You have been blessed by one of the gods of Djarat. If anyone, or anything, talks to you in ancient Djaratian, you will be able to understand the language and communicate in it. To do this, if you are ever spoken to in Djaratian, add 30 to the paragraph you are reading at the time and turn immediately to the new paragraph. For now, regain 1 LUCK point. There is nothing more for you at the Shrine of Khunam, god of knowledge and learning, so you proceed deeper into the tomb. Turn to **374**.

7

You move the piece sideways to the left, and Nemset moves White Two, two squares foward. Black One is now free to move. Will you move Black One (turn to **80**) or Black Two again (turn to **243**)?

8

After meandering through barren, rocky hills, the track descends through a boulder-strewn pass and divides, one branch continuing north-eastwards, while the other leads directly towards a line of several high peaks in the east. Looking at Jerran's map, you see that the route you are now on goes towards the temple, while the new path to the right should take you to the Shaman at Spirit Rock. Will you continue north-eastwards (turn to **146**) or take the right-hand fork (turn to **79**)?

9

It is not long before you come to the top of another flight of stone steps; at their base, you enter a large, rubble-strewn chamber, its ceiling some ten metres above you. Turn to **202**.

10

You dodge the man's charge, then draw your sword to defend yourself. He unsheathes his rusted weapon and turns on you, shouting, 'Die, Demon! You cannot prevail against the honour of Don Huan Fernandez, Knight of Vastille!' With that, the two of you engage in combat.

FERNANDEZ   SKILL 7   STAMINA 7

If you reduce your opponent's STAMINA score to 3 points or less, turn immediately to **253**.

11

The path you are following leads towards a narrow, steep-sided gorge, the land on either side of it rising up to the cliff-tops. If you have Cranno's Warning written on your *Adventure Sheet*, turn to **310**. Otherwise, turn to **298**.

12

The walls of the tunnel here are constructed from chiselled blocks of stone. Not far along the passage, you come to a place where the ceiling opens into a shaft travelling upwards, back towards the upper levels of the tomb. The tunnel also continues ahead of you. Do you want to try to climb up into the shaft in order to explore it further (turn to **352**), or do you prefer to carry on along the tunnel, in the hope of reaching your goal (turn to **299**)?

13

'I judge you worthy to enter the City of the Dead,' the Sphinx says. 'The Cult of the Cobra have taken Akharis's mummified body to the Temple of Sithera on the far side of the Necropolis, where they intend to raise him to life once more. Now go on your way.' Without hesitation, you leave the entrance hall through a second set of double doors.

You find yourself standing at a vantage point overlooking the vast Necropolis. As far as your eye can see are the stone tombs of Djaratian rulers and nobles, as well as shrines to their beast-headed gods, eldritch fires burning round the city making it all visible. The ruined Necropolis is obviously in use again. To your left lie several low stone buildings that do not appear to be tombs; to the right, in the distance, you can see what appears to be a collection of simple dwellings, possibly the ruined remains of a village. However, the edifice that dominates the complex is a great black pyramid towering over the Necropolis; a voice inside your head tells you that this is the Temple of Sithera. What will you do now?

Explore the low stone buildings?   Turn to **56**

Investigate the ruined village?   Turn to **197**

Make straight for the Temple of
Sithera?   Turn to **92**

14

The door opens easily. You enter an empty room, leading into an inner sanctum. In the centre of the sanctum stands a rectangular column and resting in a niche in its side is an exquisite golden image of a crocodile-headed man, probably a god, no more than thirty centimetres high, dressed in Djaratian garb. There is no sign of any guards, so will you take the statue (turn to **255**) or leave the shrine undisturbed and return to the tunnel (turn to **284**)?

15

Between them, the merchants have some very interesting items for sale: they are listed below with their prices. If you decide to buy anything, do so, then turn to the relevant paragraph to find out more about your new acquisition.

Oil of Lotus – 4 Gold Pieces   Turn to **155**
Two Yokka Eggs – 6 Gold Pieces   Turn to **291**
Sandworm's Tooth – 6 Gold Pieces   Turn to **328**
Alabaster Scarab – 7 Gold Pieces   Turn to **41**
Crystal Pyramid – 5 Gold Pieces   Turn to **209**

When you have finished here, you leave the market and set out on your quest; turn to **242**.

16

The passage ends at a flight of steps. Descending these, you are surprised to find yourself in a partially flooded network of tunnels. As this is the only way onwards, you wade into the water; it only comes up to your waist, so at least your provisions will remain dry. The flooding is caused by the once great river, which used to run through the desert kingdom of Djarat before its destruction but which now flows underground. Further along the tunnel you come to an intersection. Will you go straight on (turn to **217**), turn left (turn to **124**) or right (turn to **234**)?

17

You fall only a few metres and fortunately suffer nothing worse than cuts and bruises (deduct 2 points from your STAMINA). If you want to attempt the ascent of Spirit Rock again, turn to **391**. If you prefer to abandon your search for the Shaman and set off in search of the temple again, turn to **178**.

18

There are two ways you can use fire as a weapon. The first is to fight using a torch, if you have one. If you do this, turn to **138** and fight as normal, but with your Attack Strength reduced by 1 point; if you win an Attack Round, you will cause 4 points of damage to the Mummy's STAMINA rather than the usual 2, since your weapon ignites its bone-dry bandages. The second method is to throw a fire source, such as a lamp, a Yokka Egg or a burning skin of oil at the Mummy. For each one you attack in this way you must *Test your Skill*; if you succeed, the Mummy bursts into flames and is destroyed. You may try this method as many times as you have fire sources to use. Once you have used up all your fire sources, or when you give up this method of attack, note down how many of the Mummies you have already killed and turn to **138**.

19

The scarab symbol slides easily into the wall. Will you press the snake next (turn to **157**) or the vulture (turn to **230**)?

20

So now you know the location of Akharis's tomb!
Without further delay, you begin to make your way
out of the temple ruins so as to continue your journey
eastwards. Walking between the columns, you suddenly catch a glimpse of a red-robed figure dashing
behind a crumbling wall. Could it be . . .? You give
chase and, rounding the corner, see the man standing,
ten metres away, his scarlet robes bearing the golden
image of a cobra. Swiftly you draw your sword, ready
to deal with the evil cultist. However, before you can
get any closer, the man strikes the sandy bank by him
several times with the staff he is holding in his hands.
Immediately you hear an angry buzzing as a cloud
of desert wasps flies out of a hole in the bank, their
nest having been disturbed. You watch as the hornet-
like insects swarm towards the cultist, then suddenly
stop, hovering in mid-air. The cultist has his fingertips
pressed to his temple and appears to be concentrating
deeply. The wasps mass together into a cloud which
rapidly takes on the form of one of the insects, only
many times larger. The swarm, looking like a gigantic
wasp with a tapered abdomen and a sting half a metre
long, turns on its massive wings and moves towards
you threateningly. You are going to have to deal with
the swarm; there is no way of escaping it. Will you
defend yourself with your sword (turn to **222**) or will
you use an alternative weapon (turn to **108**)?

21

You pull the stakes out of the ground so that the
Dracon can free itself from the net. 'At last,' the

creature growls in a haughty tone. 'I suppose I owe you my thanks. I don't know how I ever managed to get into such a predicament in the first place. I only lay down for a nap and then those impudent trappers had the effrontery to try to capture me. No doubt I was bound for the animal traders' markets of Rimon and then into the private zoo of some upstart human noble. If there's one thing I cannot tolerate, it's a complete lack of manners.'

Four men on horseback suddenly appear between the boulders. Seeing you with their prize free, they dismount and draw their weapons. The leader of the group, stripped to the waist and with a shaven head, runs at you with a stiletto dagger grasped in one hand. You join battle with the leader while the Dracon takes on his accomplices.

TRAPPER   SKILL 8   STAMINA 7

The blade of the trapper's dagger is coated with a poison that normally induces sleep. However, it will have no such effect on you, due to your high immunity to toxins. The first time the trapper wins an Attack Round you must add 1 to your POISON total, as well as deducting the usual 2 points of damage to your STAMINA. If you win, turn to **125**.

22

It is well known that snakes fear fire, so if you have some means of clearing a path with fire, such as a skin of oil or a torch, you can use this method to reach the box easily without being bitten (turn to **186**). If you have no such items to clear the way, or if you do not wish to waste any materials necessary for such a plan, you will have to make a run for it through the asps' nest (turn to **99**).

23

As you walk towards the right-hand exit, the guards' bones rise jerkily from their posts and advance towards you. They will reach the archway before you do, so, if you want to avoid clashing with the guards, you could change direction and run through the other exit (turn to **371**). If you are intent on passing through this archway, you will have to fight.

	SKILL	STAMINA
First SKELETAL GUARD	8	6
Second SKELETAL GUARD	7	6

If you win, turn to **229**.

24

The terrain grows progressively more tortuous as you make your way towards the ruined temple. At mid-day you rest briefly, to avoid being out in the open during the hottest part of the day; but by mid-after-noon you are walking between steep cliffs and high stacks of rock. Gradually the sound of a struggle reaches your ears from somewhere to the west between the rocks. If you want to investigate, turn to **372**. If you would rather ignore the disturbance, turn to **226**.

25

You can attack the mummified animals with fire in one of two ways. The first method is to use a torch as a weapon, if you have one. To do this, turn to **163** and fight the creatures as normal but with your Attack Strength reduced by 1 point since you are using an unusual weapon; however, every successful strike you make against a creature will cause 4 points of damage to its STAMINA rather than the usual 2. The second way is to throw a fire source, such as a lamp or burning skin of oil, at a creature. For each animal, *Test your Skill* and, if you are successful, your opponent will burst into flames and be destroyed. Any you fail to destroy, or if you run out of fire sources, you will have to fight; turn to **163**. If you kill all the beasts in this way, turn to **147**.

26

You give a single loud blast on the horn and it echoes off the distant hills and across the endless sands. The two Warriors look startled — then suddenly you are aware of two more of the creatures behind you. The bone horn is one used by the Xoroa to summon help and warn the colony of danger! The mutuated ant-men close in on you from all sides. You must fight all four at the same time!

	SKILL	STAMINA
First XOROA	10	11
Second XOROA	10	10
Third XOROA	11	9
Fourth XOROA	10	11

If you somehow survive this battle, turn to **331**.

27

'To reach the deeper sections of the tomb, you will have to enter the Fangs of Sithera. The only way to escape is to locate the door-release, hidden in a corner of the room.' If you ever find yourself in the Fangs of Sithera, halve the number of the paragraph you are reading at the time, then turn to the paragraph with this new number. Now return to **286**.

28

As the Black Lion slumps to the ground, a great cheer goes up from the onlookers. Jerran is not badly wounded but, because you were distracted by having to fight the deadly beast, the cultist has got away. You will now have to try to head him off on the way to the tomb (turn to **242**) or give up the chase and visit the markets, to prepare for your quest (turn to **112**).

29

'And now my final question,' says the Sphinx. 'How many hazards must a dead person face on his or her journey through the underworld?' If you know the answer, turn to the paragraph with the same number. If you do not, you say just anything; turn to **361**.

30

The pillar-filled hall is deserted. At the far end a pair of cedar-wood doors stand ajar. Peering through them, you see another passage leading left and right. Which way will you go: to the left (turn to **87**) or to the right (turn to **254**)?

31

The night is numbingly cold and you are barely able to sleep at all. In the morning you feel worse than you did when you settled down the night before (deduct 2 points from your STAMINA). As the feeling returns to your limbs with the rising sun's warming rays, you consult Jerran's map; it shows you that you must now head directly north for the temple. Turn to **5**.

32

Your body feels as if it is being crushed, and you look down to see that you are trapped within the constricting coils of an enormous golden cobra. It raises its head until it is level with your face, and watches you with glittering eyes. And then it strikes. Your adventure is over.

33

Full of trepidation, you step over the blood-stained sand and round the great carcasses and enter the tomb. Turn to **204**.

34

The key turns in the lock and the ornate stone door swings open. You are at the top of a wide stone staircase; descending it, you enter a vast, high-ceilinged chamber. The blue roof is dotted with stylized yellow stars, while the walls are covered in plaster which has been painted with scenes of the dead king's life. In one frieze he venerates his dark goddess, in another he dictates his harsh law, and in another he communes with vile, demonic creatures. Several archways lead out of this main chamber, allowing you glimpses of fabulous golden treasures and caskets brimming with sparkling jewels.

However, your attention is drawn to Akharis's huge stone sarcophagus and the enormous serpent wrapped round it. Covered in red, black and yellow scales, the gigantic snake must be at least twenty metres long! As your light falls on to its body, the serpent's ancient, reptilian eyes flick open. Slowly it raises its head and starts to uncoil itself, its hard skin grating against the stone of the coffin as it rubs across it. With fangs as long as your arm, dripping with venom, the Great Serpent attacks.

GREAT SERPENT   SKILL   8   STAMINA 11

If the serpent wins an Attack Round, you must lose 3 STAMINA points and gain 2 POISON points from its terrible bite. If the monster wins two consecutive Attack Rounds, turn to **193**. If you kill the over-grown reptile, turn to **88**.

35

You leap through the archway just as the statue crashes to the floor behind you, completely blocking the way back into the chamber! You will never be able to move the colossus, so you descend deeper into the tomb. Turn to **216**.

36

With the cultist dead, the glowing sphere she was using to light her way fades. Ignoring this, you look around to see what else you can find. The cultist was recovering a small earthenware jar, which (as you learn when removing its lid) contains a peculiarly shaped, mummified object. If you want to take this jar, add it to your *Adventure Sheet*. You find nothing else of use to you, but then you notice that the sphere is still pulsing with faint light. If you want to pick it up, turn to **159**. If you do not, you leave the chamber; turn to **9**.

37

A quarter of an hour later, a group of four men on horseback appears between the boulders, one stripped to the waist and with a shaven head, apparently the leader. Dismounting, they approach the Dracon, which roars in defiance and fear. Unperturbed, the bald man walks up to the monster and plunges a stiletto dagger into its side. The creature soon stops struggling and falls, unconscious. The four men pull up the stakes and, having bound the Dracon's feet together, drag it on to a wooden sled pulled by two of the horses and, remounting, ride away southwards. There is nothing for you to do here but return to the trail and set off again eastwards. Turn to **250**.

38

Pulling the iron wand from your backpack, you strike Akharis with it. At once he is surrounded by a shimmering black aura — and he seems to revel in it. You are wielding the Sceptre of Oset, which the ancient Djaratian people hid from the Cult of the Cobra because it was imbued with evil power. Rather than weakening the Mummy, it has strengthened him! Remember to add 1 point to Akharis's SKILL and 3 points to his STAMINA when you come to fight him. Now turn to **215**.

39

Walking towards the mounds, you catch sight of two bizarre-looking creatures among the boulders. From the waist up they appear to be human, except that their eyes are silver and, instead of outer ears, two flexible, ant-like feelers extend forward from the top of their heads. However, their lower bodies and legs are those of a giant ant! Coloured a light reddish brown and standing about one and a half metres tall, these creatures are Xoroa. As well as being able to see in the dark, Xoroa have an acute sense of smell and they can easily pick up your scent, which is rather strong after days of sweaty travel through the scorching wilderness. The two Workers start to make a series of frantic clicks and hums, then they scuttle towards an opening in one of the mounds. Suddenly two more Xoroa appear from between the boulders. These creatures are larger than the Workers, standing almost two metres tall, and their skin is slightly darker coloured. Both are holding javelins, and one also carries a sling. Quickly the Xoroa Warrior lets fly a stone directly at you. Roll one dice. If the number rolled is odd, turn to **263**; if it is even, turn to **357**.

40

The passage turns sharply to the left and you can see a light being cast from round the corner. Carefully poking your head round the turning, you see a red-swathed figure bending over a hole in a derelict room. It is one of the cultists! Round her lie the charred outlines of three humanoid creatures, although their fanged, skull-like visages still remain. The cultist is lifting something out of the hole. Do you want to rush in and attack (turn to **212**), wait and watch for a moment (turn to **116**) or, seeing that this is a dead-end, return along the passage and go the other way (turn to **9**)?

41

The scarab, carved from a lump of veined alabaster, is actually an ancient lucky charm. Whenever you are instructed to *Test your Luck*, you may deduct 1 from the dice roll. Now return to **15**.

42

It is no good. You search desperately for a means of escape but can find none. Deep underground, Akharis's burial chamber acquires a new occupant as you are buried alive under the sand!

43

Peering round the edge of the arch, you look into a small chamber which is faced with stone; its walls are covered in hieroglyphs and carvings of animal-headed people. Standing in front of a statue of a bull-headed man that reaches up to the ceiling is a red-robed figure: the cultist you chased into the tomb! Will you enter the chamber and attack him immediately (turn to **191**) or wait to find out what the cultist is doing (turn to **340**)?

44

Nandibears have no need of treasure, so they usually remove it from their homes. However, you do find part of a human skeleton, still wearing what was once a red robe; on one bony finger is a gold ring, fashioned to look like a coiled cobra. If you want to take the Cobra Ring, make a note of it on your *Adventure Sheet*. You also find a few Gold Pieces lying among the carcasses (roll one dice to learn how many). Finding nothing else of value, you leave the Nandibear's lair and rejoin the trail leading north-westwards (turn to **337**).

45

Slowly, using the Papyrus Scroll, you are able to translate the hieroglyphs copied into the diary. The inscription reads:

> And all those who would despoil the shrine of Cracca, Lord of Rivers and Ferryman of the Gods, beware the wrath of the crocodile-headed one.

Turn to **226**.

46

The force of your blow sends Akharis reeling back into the one brazier left standing. Instantly the magical fire ignites his wrappings and the Mummy bursts into flames. Howling, Akharis's burning undead body stumbles forward and topples down the steps. In moments, all that is left of the evil creature is a pile of ashes. Akharis is truly dead at last.

But even though you have succeeded in your quest, will you be able to escape and live to tell the tale? For the first time, you notice, behind the broken remains of the statute of Sithera, an alcove which contains some of the cult's magical artefacts. Will you waste no more precious moments and flee the temple (turn to **2**), or will you see if you can use the artefacts to help you get out (turn to **232**)?

47

'That is correct,' Lopar murmurs. 'Now sit, and I shall tell you what I know of the Cult of the Cobra and the

Curse of Akharis.' You sit opposite the dog-headed Shaman and listen to his tale. 'The Cult of the Cobra are followers of Sithera, the ancient Djaratian Goddess of Evil. Sithera is, in fact, the Demon Prince Sith in the guise of a four-armed woman with a snake's head. The Djaratians worshipped many of our gods and demi-gods in the form of animal-headed humans, such as the cat goddess Meerar whom they knew as Seket, Goddess of Joy. The Djaratians also believed strongly in the power of charms. The Cult of the Cobra practise the curse-magic of their long-dead high priests, and you will no doubt need amulets and talismans to protect you from their spells.' You ask Lopar how he knows so much about the sect and the history of Djarat. 'I was not always as I appear now,' he says, sombrely. 'When I was a foolish young scholar with a lust for knowledge, searching in the desert I stumbled upon some of the ruins of that once great civilization. I filled my mind with everything and anything I could discover about the race, but I pried too far and disturbed the resting place of a high priestess of Sithera. Inadvertently I released her spirit into the world and suffered her cruel vengeance, before I managed to banish her spectre. However, if you do not stop the Cult, and if Akharis should be returned to this world, the fate of hundreds of innocent people will be much worse than mine. Do all you can to thwart their nefarious plans!' If you have any items in your possession that you wish to ask Lopar about, turn to **194**. Otherwise, the Shaman says to you: 'Now lie down beside this fire and sleep. You still have a long way to go before you meet your destiny.' Turn to **76**.

48

Swimming towards you are two huge reptiles, each four metres long. When they are very close to you, the crocodiles open their jaws wide and attack, intent on satisfying their voracious appetites. In the narrow passageway, fight the creatures one at a time. However, because you are fighting waist-deep in water, you must reduce your Attack Strength by 1 for the duration of this battle.

	SKILL	STAMINA
First CROCODILE	8	7
Second CROCODILE	7	8

The crocodile is sacred to Akharis's cult because it is such an efficient killer. There are more crocodiles guarding these flooded corridors so, if you win this battle and come to this spot again, roll one dice. If you roll 1–3, you will meet only one crocodile; on a roll of 4–5, you will meet two more; and if you roll a 6 you will meet nothing. Turn to **287**.

49

As you hit the ground, the Yokka Eggs in your backpack break. At once they hatch, releasing the fiery birds. For each egg you break, deduct one dice worth of damage from your STAMINA as the blazing creatures bathe your body in flames. If you survive, turn to **202**.

50

Keeping your back against one of the tall pillars, you are able to fight the Caarth one at a time.

	SKILL	STAMINA
CAARTH WARRIOR	10	10
CAARTH SORCERER	9	8

The first time you are hit by either of the Caarth, you must add 1 to your POISON score, as well as losing the usual 2 points from your STAMINA, because of the venom with which the evil Snakemen coat their weapons. If you win and you did not suffer any damage from the Caarth, regain 1 LUCK point and turn to **231**. If you did suffer some damage, roll one dice. On a roll of 6, turn to **158**; otherwise, turn to **231**.

51

Unsheathing your weapon, you charge at the undead horde. *Test your Luck*. If you are Lucky, turn to **138**. If you are Unlucky, turn to **176**.

52

The Cyclops falls to the ground, dead. If Fernandez attacked you when you last met, turn to **261**. If he did not, turn to **96**.

53

You become engrossed in the game, forgetting your worries for a while. Soon the board looks like this:

As you can see, the piece, Black One, is trapped at the moment by White One and White Two. It is your turn; which piece will you move?

Black Two?	Turn to **7**
Black Three?	Turn to **156**
Black Four?	Turn to **205**
Black Five?	Turn to **184**

54

Where will you go now: through the other door, if you have not already been there (turn to **393**), or along the new passage leading away from this junction (turn to **239**)?

55

Before you can get to your feet, you feel the cultist's hands round your throat (deduct 2 points from your STAMINA). The cultist is trying to strangle you! Fight the battle which follows in the normal way; however, you cannot injure your opponent until you have got free. If you win an Attack Round, do not deduct any points from his STAMINA score. If you win two consecutive Attack Rounds, you manage to free yourself from the cultist's grip and, from then onwards, you can injure the cultist in the usual way.

CULTIST   SKILL 7   STAMINA 7

If you win, turn to **214**.

56

An eerie silence pervades this area of the city. Inside the buildings you find rooms containing stone tables and benches covered with rusty tools and broken clay pots. In the heart of the complex you enter one room that has been used recently: scraps of linen lie, discarded, on the floor and a dark fluid has stained the crumbling slab. It is then you realize the purpose of these rooms: these are the embalming chambers to which the bodies of the dead were brought to be preserved. You are especially interested in two jars, half-full of strange liquids. One is sweet-smelling, while the other stinks foully and is syrupy. Do you want to:

Drink some of the sweet-smelling
  liquid? Turn to **82**
Drink some of the reeking syrup? Turn to **173**
Rub some of the syrup on your skin? Turn to **219**
Leave the embalming chambers? Turn to **147**

57

You react immediately, sprinting through the gorge away from the landslide, although you are still hit by a few small rocks (deduct 2 points from your STAMINA). Turn to **89**.

58

Gazing into the depths of the crystal orb, you concentrate all your mental energies into searching for something within it. *Test your Skill*, adding 1 to the dice roll. If you succeed, turn to **358**. If you fail, turn to **313**.

59

When the Death Spider bites you, it also injects its poison into your bloodstream, paralysing you. The Demon drags your body on to its web and goes on biting you until you are dead. Its dire task complete, the Death Spider, along with its web and your corpse, dematerializes, returning to the Realms of the Damned, where your soul will be extracted and tortured for all eternity!

60

The lapis lazuli set into the breastplate glows with an inner light and above you hovers a great spirit falcon, its wings scintillating with azure flames. The bird of prey swoops down on the phantasmal creature and tears at the beast with its ghostly talons, while the snake-heads strike at the falcon. Within seconds the battle is over and the jackal-spirit is banished back to the Demonic Planes. Its duty done, the falcon also vanishes.

Suddenly you feel the priestess's gaze upon you. Her eyes burn with a crimson fire, and under her cruel stare you feel the strength ebbing from your body. If you have an Eye-shaped Amulet, turn to **151**. If you do not, turn to **344**.

61

Finding itself being overwhelmed by your superior fighting skill, the Dracon leaps out of reach of your weapon and takes to the air on its stubby wings. As it flies away, it continues to hurl insults at you until it is out of earshot. Alone again, you continue on your quest. Turn to **250**.

62

These desolate highlands seem to be devoid of life in any form; you make your way further to the east under the glare of the blazing sun, but there is still no sign of the cultist. The route you are following climbs upwards until you are walking along a narrow path bounded on your right by a steep, rocky slope and on your left by a precipice. Without warning, a surprisingly cold wind begins to blow in from across the desert, swirling the sand round about you. As you watch, the spiralling current of air and sand becomes a focused column and forms a recognizable shape. Standing on the track in front of you is a humanoid, over two metres in height and composed entirely of the substance of the desert. With great clenched fists and a malevolent red glow in its eye-sockets, the Sand Golem advances on you. What will you use against this magical creation:

Your sword?	Turn to **143**
Firepowder or a Yokka Egg?	Turn to **81**
The statuette of a god?	Turn to **378**
A Sandworm's Tooth?	Turn to **308**
A Carved Bone Horn?	Turn to **220**

63

Passing the door from the Decayer's chamber, and the entrance to this level of the tomb, you soon come upon a stone door, without a handle, in the left-hand wall. You try pushing against the door but can find no way of opening it. Then you notice an inscription carved round the door. If you want to stop for a while and translate the message using the papyrus scroll, turn to **198**. Otherwise, you will have to press on as you can find no way of opening the door (turn to **374**).

64

Unstoppering the bottle, you throw its contents over the Mummy. Akharis howls with pain as the purifying waters eat into his undead body like acid! Roll one dice: this is how much damage the Waters of Life cause the Mummy (make a note of the number of points of STAMINA loss you have already inflicted on Akharis). Turn to **215**.

65

Buried under the piles of bones you unearth the remains of a backpack that you presume belonged to the unfortunate human. Looking inside the backpack, you find a small notebook. Opening it, you discover that it is a diary or journal. From what you can make out, its owner was among the band of explorers, one of whom tumbled into Jerran Farr's camp eight days ago; the diary contains information about their progress to the temple, but you also read something else of interest. On their journey the group came upon some ruins which they believed to be Djaratian. On one section of wall they found an inscription in a strange picture script; it is reproduced in the diary. There is nothing else of interest, but before leaving you decide to take the Rasaur's two eggs with you, each of which will provide a meal in itself (add 2 to your Provisions). Turn to **226**.

66

You try wedging your backpack between the roof and one corner of the room, but to no effect. Next you try your sword, but this snaps under the inexorable pressure of the descending ceiling. Finally you lie down and brace yourself against the floor, pushing against the ceiling with your legs, but even this desperate measure makes no difference. The Fangs of Sithera claim their first victim in several thousand years.

67

You raise the stone easily. Beneath it you find a shallow storage pit. In this are some decayed provisions and a peculiar, wand-like object, made of iron, that has remained untarnished in this dry atmosphere; its end is fashioned in the shape of a clawed hand. If you want to take the iron wand, add it to your *Adventure Sheet*. Whether you do or not, you will now have to leave the village. Where will you make for now: the Temple of Sithera (turn to **92**) or the low stone buildings, if you haven't been there already (turn to **56**)?

68

Fortunately, since you are standing back-to-back in the narrow street, only one cultist can attack each of you at a time. You prepare to defend yourself against the leader.

CULTIST   SKILL 7   STAMINA 7

If you defeat your opponent, turn to **214**.

69

The tangle of flooded corridors you are in now leads off in all directions. Peering down new intersecting tunnels, you see that yet more passageways lead off from these. Which way will you go?

First left, first right, second right?	Turn to **217**
First right, first left, then straight on?	Turn to **162**
Second right, then straight on?	Turn to **182**
Second left, first right?	Turn to **301**

70

Using the incredible strength of your willpower alone, you break the control of the Path of Fear. The terror of the waking nightmare was all in your mind. Now the corridor is empty once more and you can continue on your way, but you have been permanently scarred by the experience. Reduce both your *Initial* and current SKILL by 1 point. Turn to **16**.

71

Peering through the archway, you find yourself looking into a small chamber faced with stone; its walls are covered in hieroglyphs and carvings of animal-headed people. On the opposite side of the room is a statue of a bull-headed man that reaches up to the ceiling. Your flickering light casts eerie shadows across the walls and you decide that there is nothing here of any importance to your quest, so you continue along the tunnel. Eventually the passage turns right again, bringing you to the top of another flight of stone steps. You have no choice but to descend, wondering how far down into the earth this tomb leads. Turn to **216**.

72

Muscles tensed, you spring forward and manage to get hold of the statue. Where you were standing a moment ago is now the opening into a pit of bubbling acid! Pulling yourself to safety, you put the Malachite Amulet round your neck and waste no time in getting out of the room. Turn to **247**.

73

No matter what you try to use against the statue, your attempts to stop it are futile. A massive stone foot is raised and then smashed down with tremendous force, with you underneath it. Your adventure ends here.

74

Unrolling the scroll, you see that it is covered in incomprehensible hieroglyphic picture-script, written in black ink and arranged into five columns. You can make no sense of the hieroglyphs, so you roll the scroll up again and tuck it into your backpack. Return to **339**.

75

Walking along the sand-strewn tunnel, the passageway eventually turns ninety degrees to the left, then continues as before. As you progress further you see that ahead of you, to the right, part of the tunnel wall has caved in, revealing the entrance to a roughly circular tunnel. As you approach, you can hear scuttling and scraping sounds coming from the hole. A huge, glossy-brown, oval-bodied beetle enters the passageway, rolling a large ball of compacted earth and stones in front of it. Then the Giant Scarab stops, sensing your presence, and clicks its mandibles menacingly. You have invaded the beetle's territory and are blocking its path. With one tremendous push, the Scarab sends the ball of earth hurtling directly at you. *Test your Skill*. If you succeed, turn to **246**. If you fail, turn to **172**.

76

You wake up as the sun is rising over the eastern hills. You are lying in the middle of a dusty track that wends its way north-westwards through the wilderness. Behind you, many kilometres away on the horizon, you can see the silhouette of Spirit Rock. Lopar has helped you once more on your quest (regain 1 LUCK point and 2 STAMINA points). With renewed vigour you proceed on your way.

Under Glantanka's unrelenting gaze you travel on through the heat of the day. The uneven path leads you further into the wilderness that fringes the Desert of Skulls. You follow the route north-westwards across boulder-strewn hills and through narrow valleys. As you pass through one rocky gully you notice a large hole at its base, leading underground. Do you want to stop and investigate this entrance into the earth (turn to 324) or will you continue on your way without hesitation (turn to 226)?

77

You squeeze through the small hole and crawl along a tunnel on your belly for a few metres. The tunnel suddenly slopes steeply downwards and you find yourself sliding into the depths of the temple. The tunnel eventually opens into a bare chamber and you are deposited on the hard stone floor. An archway leads out of this chamber and further into the temple, so this is the way you will have to go. Turn to 347.

78

You know you cannot harm the Sentinel of the Shrine unless you are in contact with a piece of the material from which it is formed. However, while retrieving this item you are vulnerable to attack and must automatically lose the first round of combat. After that you can fight on as normal.

GOLDEN SENTINEL   SKILL 11   STAMINA 12

If you win, turn to 368.

79

As the sun reaches its highest point, you rest for a few minutes in the shade of a great slab of rock. (You may eat Provisions here if you wish.) The whole landscape looks as if a Giants' game of knuckle-bones has been played here. The only signs of life in this scorching wilderness are the occasional lizard, running over the rocks in search of beetles, and a lonely bird of prey soaring on the warm thermals above you in the cloudless azure sky. The only sound is made by a cool breeze blowing through the valley . . . but it isn't the only sound! You are suddenly aware of a low growling coming from somewhere among the rocks behind you. Do you want to investigate the source of this noise (turn to **294**), or will you hurriedly move on eastwards again (turn to **250**)?

80
It is a close thing, but Nemset's piece just beats yours to the opposite end of the board. You concede defeat and prepare to leave the tomb. Turn to **322**.

81
There is a sudden blinding flash and, as your eyes recover, you are startled by the sight now in front of you. Under the intense heat of the explosion produced by your attack the sand that the Golem was composed of has completely vitrified. Standing on the path in front of you know is a motionless glass statue. You give the Golem one great push and it plummets over the edge of the precipice, smashing into hundreds of pieces when it hits the rocks below. Regain 1 LUCK point for your quick thinking and turn to **183**.

82
You gulp the liquid down and discover that it is wine infused with medicinal herbs. The wine is used to

clean the corpse before it is mummified, but on you it has a restorative effect (regain up to 4 STAMINA points and increase your Attack Strength by 1 point during your next battle). Now will you:

Drink some of the foul-smelling syrup?	Turn to **173**
Rub some of the syrup on your body?	Turn to **219**
Leave the embalming chambers?	Turn to **379**

83

Yokka Eggs are warm to the touch; with one of these clutched to you while you sleep you will not need to light a fire. The night passes peacefully without any disturbances (restore 2 STAMINA points). In the morning, having consulted Farr's map again, you take a route north towards the temple; turn to **5**.

84

You reach out a hand to pick up a fistful of jewels but jump back in surprise as the treasure pile rears up in front of you. You blink several times and the illusion disappears. The room is actually home to a Scitalis, a large, brightly coloured snake which traps its prey with illusions of treasure. You are going to have to fight the deceiving serpent, but at least you can take some comfort from the fact that its bite is not poisonous – it does not need to be!

SCITALIS   SKILL 8   STAMINA 10

If you win, turn to **3**.

85

What will you use: a Bronze Rattle (turn to **168**), an Iron Wand (turn to **38**) or the Book of the Dead (turn to **245**)? If you have none of these items, turn to **215**.

86

'The great Cranno, hero of a hundred tragedies, has no time to help lesser mortals when he has a dozen soliloquies to rehearse. Now leave this place.' Will you do as the man says (turn to **8**) or attack him (turn to **134**)?

87

You wander along the featureless tunnel – one corridor is very like another in this labyrinthine tomb. Eventually, having led you around to the right, the passage does reveal something of interest. To your left is the entrance to another passage, but it has been crudely blocked with lumps of rock. It may take a while but you think you can clear the obstruction. Do you want to:

Clear the entrance by hand?	Turn to **166**
Use Firepowder, if you have some, to clear it?	Turn to **390**
Continue along the passage?	Turn to **154**

88

With the serpent dead, will you open the sarcophagus immediately (turn to **376**), or do you want to search Akharis's treasure-rooms first (turn to **179**)?

89

As the dust clears, you hear a terrible shriek and look up at the rocky ledges above you. On both sides of the gorge, among the rocks, is a group of six baboons. They are almost as large as men, covered in bristly fur and with vicious-looking, sharp teeth. They are leaping up and down, snarling and howling cruelly. One, larger than the rest, is standing on its hind legs and holding a boulder over its head. It must have been these creatures which caused the landslide. Sensing that the baboons will attack at any moment, you unsheathe your sword – and not a moment too soon, as the two nearest apes leap towards you, ready to tear you to pieces with their clawed hands. Fight them both together.

	SKILL	STAMINA
First BABOON	7	5
Second BABOON	6	6

If you kill the vicious creatures, turn to **316**.

90

As you reach the top of yet another ridge you pass an outcrop of rock, and suddenly your goal becomes visible. At the edge of a vast mesa that stretches to the east and north, rising up between two of the sandy hills is a tall pinnacle of rock, its sides almost vertical. A massive boulder, which appears to be precariously balanced, rests on its flat top. The boulder is covered in swirling patterns formed by veins of some crystalline substance. There is a strong aura of elemental energy about the place and a voice inside your head tells you that this must be Spirit Rock. A thin trail of smoke rises into the air from the top of the boulder, and you can just make out a small cave entrance at its base where it rests on the pinnacle. The Shaman must live at the top of the rock and, from all appearances, you assume that he is there at the moment. However, the only way you are going to gain access to the cave is to scale the pinnacle. If you are determined to seek the Shaman's aid and want to make the dangerous climb, turn to **152**. If you would rather abandon this approach and set off in search of the temple once more, turn to **178**.

91

'By Assamarra, God of the Sands, I command you to begone!' As soon as you have spoken these words, the wind picks up again, but this time it blows the Golem's insubstantial, shifting form apart, scattering the sand throughout the wilderness. The deity of deserts and arid places himself has aided you. Regain 1 LUCK point and turn to **183**.

92

Making your way along the processional avenue of the Necropolis, you see the black pyramid looming up in front of you. However, before you reach the temple, you pass through other areas of the city that may be of interest. To your left, extending towards the distant edge of the cavern are the tombs of Djaratians, while to the right are shrines to their gods. Do you want to proceed by making for:

The tombs?	Turn to **149**
The shrines?	Turn to **295**
The Temple of Sithera?	Turn to **395**

93

You fall more than twenty metres down the side of the pinnacle, hitting rocky outcrops and ledges on the way down. You land heavily among the boulders at the base of Spirit Rock, seriously injured; you are covered in cuts and bruises; you have several cracked ribs and have sprained your left ankle (deduct 7 points from your STAMINA, 2 points from your SKILL and 1 point from your LUCK). You are no longer in any condition to climb the rock so, having tended to your wounds, you set off, hobbling in great pain, for the temple. Turn to **178**.

94

The Decayer bursts into flames on contact with the source of your fire and is soon consumed by fire. You carefully avoid the undead creature as it stumbles about in the chamber, screeching, and deftly move towards the door. Turn to **148**.

95

'Your second question. In reaching the Necropolis you have ferried yourself across the Sacred Lake. But tell me this: who is the Ferryman of the Gods and Lord of Rivers?' Convert the name of the deity that is the answer into numbers, using the code A = 1, B = 2, C = 3 ... Z = 26. Add the numbers together then turn to the paragraph with the same number as the total you have calculated. If you get it wrong, or if you do not know the answer, turn to **262**.

96

'Thank you, my friend,' says the old knight. 'You are a truly noble and honourable warrior. Between us we have rid the land of one of the foul giant brethren. Let us drink a toast together. Gordo!' he calls. 'Where are you, man?' Fernandez's cowardly manservant emerges from his hiding place and approaches his master. 'Give me the bottle of Old Sarnak's we've got,' the old man tells him. 'Here, my friend,' he says, passing you the bottle, 'this will revitalize your spirits.' You take a swig of the fortified wine and immediately feel its effects. Restore up to 4 STAMINA points and add 1 point to your Attack Strength for the next combat you are involved in. While Gordo tends Don Huan's wounds, you waste no more time in returning to your original route to the temple. Turn to **226**.

97

At last you find yourself face-to-face with the ancient evil that you came all this way to destroy. Remember to deduct any points of SKILL or STAMINA damage you may have already caused the Mummy, then do battle with Akharis, who tries to beat you into oblivion with his powerful fists.

AKHARIS   SKILL 13   STAMINA 25

If you overcome your inhumanly strong, ultimate opponent, turn to **336**.

98

A short figure suddenly appears in the open doorway. The man is dressed in plain grey robes and is wearing a mask with grotesquely exaggerated features. 'I am the great Cranno, master of a thousand roles, possessor of a thousand guises!' the little man booms. Will you:

Ask Cranno for his help?	Turn to **304**
Attack him?	Turn to **134**
Leave the theatre?	Turn to **8**

99

Roll one dice and add 1 to the total; this is the number of snakes which bite you as you pick your way over their writhing mass. For each bite, deduct 1 point from your STAMINA and, for every two bites suffered, add 1 to your POISON score as well! If you survive the venomous asps, turn to **186**.

100

Ahead of you a broad set of steps leads up out of the water and deeper into the tomb. At last you have found a way out of the flooded maze! Regain 1 LUCK point. Back on dry land, so to speak, you follow the short passage that leads away from the steps to a T-junction. To the left you can see that the tunnel ends at a stone door, while to the right it continues into darkness. Will you go to the left (turn to **165**) or to the right (turn to **12**)?

101

'There are many,' Rhehotep replies seriously. 'If you are to reach Akharis's burial chamber, you will have to confront the Guardian of the Dead and overcome it. Also, beware of Amentut, should you encounter him. He was Akharis's Vizier and is loyal even in death.' Return to **286**.

102

Unfortunately, this bizarre character does not believe the account you give of yourself. 'Why, you lying cur!' he roars. 'Where is the knightly apparel that one on a quest should wear? No, you must be some rogue who preys on helpless travellers. Or are you in fact a shape-changing Demon, sent by that confounded sorcerer Zanmethees to torment me?' The old man is clearly not thinking rationally. With a shout, he kicks his heels into his nag's sides and levels his lance at your chest. Continue as if you were conducting one round of combat to determine the Attack Strength of yourself and the madman, but do not deduct any STAMINA points (he has a SKILL of 7). If you have the higher Attack Strength, turn to **10**. If his is higher, turn to **211**.

103

What will you use against the Mummies: fire (turn to **18**) or any charms you may have (turn to **241**)? If you have none of these, you will have to use your sword (turn to **51**).

104

You have chosen wrongly in your combination. Rather than the wall opening, a great block of stone pushes out from the wall, behind the bull-god's statue. Looking up in horror, you see the great stone colossus topple forward and at the same instant you start to run. Roll three dice. If the total rolled is less than or equal to your STAMINA score, turn to **35**; if it is greater, turn to **122**.

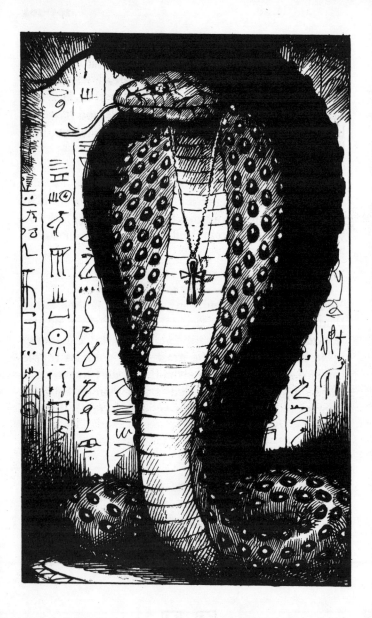

105

You soon come to an archway in the right-hand wall. Beyond it is a flagstoned chamber, decorated with yet more wall-paintings. However, your attention is drawn to a magnificent golden statue of a rearing cobra on the far side of the room. The statue, standing on a finely chiselled plinth, is two metres tall and its jewelled eyes sparkle in the flickering light. Hanging from the cobra's head is an amulet set with a piece of malachite, which may be of use against the cult's curse-magic. Do you want to enter the room, with the intention of retrieving the amulet (turn to **136**), or would you prefer to pass it by and continue along the tunnel (turn to **247**)?

106

As you flee, you hear the Dracon break free of the net and launch itself into the air. Your heart pounding, you are suddenly knocked to the ground. As you lie in the dust, trying to catch your breath, you feel blood oozing from a gash on your back (deduct 2 points from your STAMINA). The Dracon lands and stalks towards you. 'Well, puny human,' it snarls, 'let us see what you can do with that lump of iron you call a weapon!'

DRACON　　　　SKILL 9　　　　STAMINA 14

The Dracon continues to deride your skill and mock you as you fight; as a result, you must reduce your Attack Strength by 1 point for the duration of this battle. If you reduce the creature's STAMINA to 5 points or less, turn at once to **61**.

107

The diabolical creature, conjured from the underworld of Djaratian myth, leaps at you, snarling. Your earthly weapon is useless against the demonic spirit, which soon overcomes you. Your body will be sacrificed to Sithera so that Akharis may live again.

108

If you have a torch, turn to **240**. Otherwise, you may use weapons such as Firepowder or a Yokka Egg against the swarm, but in the end you will have to resort to using your sword (turn to **222**).

109

You notice a crack at the base of the sarcophagus and marks on the floor as if something heavy has been pushed across it. Desperately, you push against the immense stone coffin in the hope of revealing an escape route. Roll three dice. If the total rolled is less than or equal to your STAMINA score, turn to **290**. If it is greater, turn to **171**.

110

Using your sword, you slice the top off the plant and, removing the spines, bite into its juicy flesh. The bitter taste makes you wince and, before you know what you are doing, you have swallowed some of the liquid. As well as being protected by its spines, the Barbthorn has a second defence against would-be diners: it is poisonous. (Add 2 to your POISON total and deduct 3 points from your STAMINA.) Spitting out the rest of the plant, you hurry on your way, leaving the toxic Barbthorn behind. Turn to **11**.

111

If you cleared a path to the box using fire, the flames have now died down and you will either have to employ the same means again (remember to cross off from your *Adventure Sheet* whatever you use to clear a path through the asps), in which case you will be unharmed, or you will have to run for it. If you choose the second option, roll one dice and deduct the total from your STAMINA score, due to the snake bites; for every 2 STAMINA points you lose, add 1 to your POISON score! If you survive, or if you clear a safe path using fire, turn to 54.

112

Quickly exploring Rimon's markets, you soon discover what the many stalls have to offer. Jerran Farr hands you a bag containing 30 Gold Pieces and leaves it to you to decide what may be most useful on your quest. Read through the list of items described below and, if you buy anything, deduct the appropriate number of Gold Pieces and record the item on your *Adventure Sheet*. You may buy only one of any item on this list unless you are told otherwise.

Rope and Grapple – a length of rope with a metal hook attached at one end. Cost: 3 Gold Pieces.

Provisions – you may buy any number of meals. Cost: 1 Gold Piece per meal.

Lantern and Oil – each use of the lantern consumes one skin of oil. Cost: 2 Gold Pieces for the lantern plus one skin of oil. Additional skins: 1 Gold Piece per skin.

Healing Draught – each tot of this elixir restores STAMINA points equivalent to half your *Initial* score (rounding fractions up). There are three tots in the bottle. Cost: 5 Gold Pieces.

Anti-Poison – when drunk, this potion will reduce your POISON total by 4 points. Cost: 4 Gold Pieces.

Brass Telescope – this finely crafted telescope is one of the most incredible examples of the metalworker's art that you have ever seen. Cost: 5 Gold Pieces.

Firepowder – an alchemical compound wrapped in a paper parcel with a taper protruding from one end. When lit, within a few seconds the package will explode (roll one dice to find out how many points you may deduct from the STAMINA of any creature in contact with it). You may throw the package at an opponent at the start of a battle by successfully *Testing your Skill*. Cost: 4 Gold Pieces.

Torch – a length of wood with oil-soaked rags wrapped round one end. Useful as either a light source or a flaming weapon. You may buy a maximum of three torches. Cost: 1 Gold Piece per torch.

Several merchants, who look as if they have done very well for themselves from the trade, try to tempt you into inspecting their slightly more unusual – and more expensive – wares. If you have some money left and want to have a look at what they have to offer, turn to **15**. Otherwise, you leave the market and set off on your quest (turn to **242**).

113

You stop half-way along the corridor and begin to search for the entrance to the hidden room that Rhehotep spoke of. *Test your Skill*, adding 2 to the dice roll. If you succeed, turn to **323**. If you fail, turn to **145**.

114

Even if Don Huan Fernandez did attack you at your first meeting, the eccentric old man is just a witless fool, and leaving him to a cruel death at the hands of the Cyclops is not an action befitting a hero such as yourself (lose 1 LUCK point). Turn to **226**.

115

With grim determination, you stagger across the chamber, sweating profusely. When you are past the fires you collapse, exhausted (deduct 1 point from your STAMINA). Unable to go on for the moment after the strength-sapping heat of the Path of Flames, you sit down and rest. Ten minutes pass before you feel ready to set off once more. Getting to your feet, you march along the tunnel until you reach a door, covered in gold-leaf, to your left. Do you want to try this door (turn to **14**) or will you keep to your present path (turn to **284**)?

116

The cultist is holding a small earthenware jar, inscribed with hieroglyphs, in her hands. Now you can also see where the light in the room is coming from, for resting next to the cultist is a glowing white sphere.

As she turns to leave the room, she sees you and, picking up the sphere, hurls it at you. The blazing ball hits you in the chest and you feel its white-hot heat scorching your body (deduct 4 points from your STAMINA). Wielding her curved sword, the cultist runs at you.

CULTIST   SKILL 7   STAMINA 7

If you win, turn to 36.

117

The monster's nocturnal wanderings are not difficult to trace, and after an hour you reach a wide cave mouth in the hilly uplands. Knowing Nandibears to be solitary predators, you approach without fear of meeting the creature's mate. Entering the cave, your nostrils are assailed by a strong animal odour and the smell of rotting meat. The monster's lair is littered with half-chewed bones and shattered skulls. *Test your Luck.* If you are Lucky, turn to 44. If you are Unlucky, turn to 380.

118

Not sure what else to do, you hurl the jar on to the ground, smashing it to pieces and crushing the mummified bundle it held beneath your foot. Akharis's Mummy doubles up in agony as you do so. Of course, the preserved package must be one of Akharis's major internal organs, removed by the priests of Sithera centuries ago, as part of the embalming process. For every earthenware jar you have that you can destroy, deduct 1 point from Akharis's STAMINA; for every two jars smashed, you can also deduct 1 SKILL point from the Mummy. Now, while Akharis is weakened, will you:

Attack him with fire?	Turn to **330**
Use the Waters of Life, if you have them?	Turn to **64**
Use a charm against him?	Turn to **85**
Try to remove his death-mask?	Turn to **293**
Try to destroy the sarcophagus?	Turn to **257**
Use your sword?	Turn to **97**

119

You do not have to wait long before you notice a disturbance down in the valley. From nowhere, it seems, a sandstorm suddenly blows up but, as quickly as it appeared it dies down again; once the sand has settled, you see a red-robed figure standing at the entrance to the tomb. It is the same cultist you encountered at the temple! He looks around for a moment then disappears into the tomb. Swiftly you descend into the valley and dash across the sand, hoping to get there before the Giant Lizards notice you. *Test your Skill*, adding 2 to the dice roll. If you are successful, turn to **348**. If you fail, turn to **306**.

120

Before you leave the cavern, you set fire to the Demon's carcass and its web. Regain 1 LUCK point for defeating such a powerful opponent. Climbing back up the slope, you can either enter the pillared hall (turn to **30**) or return to the passage before that and turn left (turn to **254**)?

121

Before you can reach her, the priestess casts a spell. At once thick, green smoke begins to pour out of one of the braziers and in its midst you can see a phantasmal shape forming. The demonic spirit has the body of a huge jackal, with two dog-like heads sprouting from its shoulders. Behind them a mass of serpent bodies writhe up along its back and two scorpion tails lash menacingly behind it. Do you have a Falcon Breastplate? If you have, turn to the paragraph which is the same number as the number of feathers on the falcon; if you haven't, turn to **107**.

122

After days of trudging through the desert, your legs are just not strong enough to get you out of the chamber in time. You are only a metre from the archway when the statue crashes down on top of you, crushing the life out of your body.

123

In panic you sprint through the gorge – but, unfortunately, not quickly enough. Several rocks hit you and knock you to the ground, stunned (deduct 6 points from your STAMINA). Turn to **89**.

124

The tunnel you are following is soon joined by several others from the left and right. Will you go straight on (turn to **249**), take the first to the left (turn to **182**), the second to the left (turn to **272**), the third to the left (turn to **195**), the first to the right (turn to **301**) or the second to the right (turn to **69**)?

125

You land the fatal blow as the Dracon brings down one of the other men. The other two trappers fling themselves on to their mounts and gallop away, screaming in terror. 'It seems I owe you my thanks again,' says the creature, 'and as a sign of my gratitude I shall give you a gift.' The great beast bounds up the side of a boulder, launches itself into the air on its stubby wings, and disappears from view. You do not have to wait long, however, before the Dracon returns, holding in its mouth an object which it drops at your feet. The article is half a metre long and looks like a T-shaped cross whose top arm consists of a loop. It is made of solid gold and has twelve precious stones set into it. It must be very valuable. 'I hope you find this acceptable,' the Dracon says, 'and thank you again, human.' With that, the golden creature flaps its wings and rises into the sky, leaving you alone again to continue on your quest. Turn to **250**.

126

Wondering what else to do, you cast the powders into the magical flames of the brazier. Thick, choking, green smoke pours from the brazier and you can see, forming within it, a grotesque, demonic apparition.

The powders were used by the cult's High Priestess to commune with creatures of the Pit. However, before the summoned hellspawn can kill you, the temple roof caves in, burying you alive.

127

In one corner of the room you find a rounded granite catch. You pull it and the doorway in front of you slowly rises. Not waiting for it to open fully, you throw yourself through the gap as the spiked roof meets the floor of the chamber behind you. You have escaped the Fangs of Sithera! Regain 1 LUCK point. Picking yourself up, you look around. A few metres away is a T-junction; looking to the right, you can see a painted door, while to the left the passage is swallowed up in the darkness. Will you go to the left (turn to 105) or to the right (turn to 315)?

128

Carved from a single piece of bone, the horn is well made but is otherwise quite unremarkable. Return to 339.

129

Nemset is just too good for you – but then, she is an expert and you are just a novice – and victory is soon hers. Turn to 322.

130

The passage soon ends at the entrance to a ruined room – and now you cannot believe your eyes. Reflected in the light you are carrying is a huge pile of jewels and gold coins! There is no way onwards through the room, so will you enter and take some of the treasure (turn to **84**), leave the room and make your way along the adjoining passage, if you have not done so already (turn to **370**), or retrace your steps back along the tunnel past the door by which you entered this part of the tomb (turn to **63**)?

131

Keeping the hills to your right, you trek across the hot sands of a desert which stretches as far as you can see to the north. After almost an hour's journeying, you catch sight of several hillocks of sand, each with a large opening at its summit, close to the edge of the hills. Could these possibly be entrances to Djaratian tombs, although they are much closer than you would have expected? Do you want to investigate the mounds (turn to **39**) or will you keep well clear of them and proceed along the outskirts of the desert (turn to **189**)?

132

As you stride confidently along the avenue, the two guards see you and, before you can attempt any bluff, charge at you. They are grotesque to look at, with human bodies but savage, bestial heads, and hands gripping cruel pole-arms! Fight them both at the same time.

	SKILL	STAMINA
First TEMPLE GUARD	8	8
Second TEMPLE GUARD	8	7

If you win, you enter the black pyramid; turn to **347**.

133

'I believe that there is some such item in a hidden room close to here. Leaving this chamber, turn left, then right, and the secret entrance is around there.' If you later find yourself in this passage, you may look for the entrance to the hidden room by deducting 100 from the paragraph you are reading at the time then turning to this new paragraph. 'There is also a charm that may be of use to you in the chamber of the Golden Cobra,' Rhehotep adds. Return to **286**.

134

At a single word from the strange man, a huge Sabre-toothed Tiger bounds through the doorway and across the sand to attack you before you can reach its master.

SABRE-TOOTHED TIGER   SKILL 9   STAMINA 8

If you win, turn to **237**.

135

You think that fire may be an effective method of attack against the Decayer. If you have some means of setting the skeleton on fire, such as a torch, Yokka Eggs or a skin of oil, and you want to try this, turn to **94**. If you do not, or if you do not wish to waste a fire source (you cannot use your light, if you have nothing else, so leaving yourself in the darkness), turn to **258**.

136

Creeping towards the huge golden cobra, you prepare yourself for any devious traps that may have been set. As you step on to the last flagstone in front of the statue, it gives way beneath you. *Test your Skill*. If you are successful, turn to **72**; if you are not, turn to **206**.

137

The Scorpion dextrously evades your defences, grabs you in one of its claws and its sting whips forward. Its normally fatal poison is injected into your bloodstream, but fortunately you have built up a resistance to such toxins (add 4 to your POISON total and deduct 3 points from your STAMINA). Now return to **242** and continue your battle with the monster.

138

The Mummy horde numbers fifteen in total. With their atrophying hands outstretched in front of them, the powerful undead advance towards you. Fortunately, because Mummies are slow-moving, you can fight them one at a time. Each Mummy has SKILL 9 and STAMINA 12. (Remember to reduce the total by any you may have already destroyed.) If any individual battle lasts longer than nine Attack Rounds, turn to 236. If you manage to overcome all the shambling undead, turn to 367.

139

If you have a Carved Bone Horn, you could try blowing into it to scare off the Xoroa (turn to 26). If you have anything else you may want to use, such as a Yokka Egg or Firepowder, turn to 218 and use it before you fight the two Warriors. If you have none of the above, you will have to rely on cold steel once more (turn to 218).

140

Moving across to the archway, you direct your light into the room beyond. At the foot of a few steps, the floor of the chamber is completely covered by the glistening bodies of hundreds of asps, a small but venomous species of snake! Only six metres away, an iron box sits on top of a stone plinth. If you want to attempt to cross the room to the iron box, turn to **22**. Otherwise, you have no choice but to leave this place; turn to **54**.

141

The scarab slides easily into the wall, as does the snake after it. A grinding sound begins behind the wall and you watch expectantly for the door to open. Turn to **104**.

142

You have no idea where you are in the flooded maze. Roll one dice. If you roll:

1	Turn to **369**
2	Turn to **124**
3	Turn to **272**
4	Turn to **69**
5 or 6	Turn to **48**

143

Because of its insubstantial, shifting form, blows from your weapon pass straight through the Sand Golem and will cause it only 1 STAMINA point of damage (2 STAMINA points after a successful *Test for Luck*). However, hits from the magical creature are like punches from an iron gauntlet covered in sandpaper and will still inflict 2 STAMINA points of damage on you!

SAND GOLEM   SKILL 8   STAMINA 9

If you reduce your opponent's STAMINA to zero, you break the spell animating the Golem, and it becomes a harmless heap of sand once more (turn to **183**).

144

Something tells you to pull the Ankh out of your backpack and brandish it in front of the statue. The Ankh glows with power in your grasp. The statue's piercing gaze falls on the ancient artefact and it stops in its tracks. Then the stone limbs stiffen once more and the eldritch light of its eyes fades. Screaming with fury, the cultists run towards you, intent on avenging themselves by your demise. But the transformation of the statue is not over yet. With a terrible cracking sound, fissures appear all over Sithera's image and pieces of it break off and fall to the floor of the chamber. At the same time, great rifts form across the walls of the dark temple and huge chunks of masonry crash down all round you. The whole temple is starting to collapse! The cultists forget about you and, more concerned over their own plight, try to flee from the crumbling building. Just as you are thinking of following suit, two rotting hands reach out and grab you round the neck. Unravaged by fire, Akharis lives again! Breaking free of the Mummy's grip, you must now fight Akharis again.

AKHARIS   SKILL 8   STAMINA 10

If you reduce Akharis's STAMINA score to 4 points or less in five Attack Rounds or fewer, turn to **46**. If you do not, before your battle is even over the temple roof falls in, crushing you under tonnes of rock.

145

Try as you may, you cannot find any hidden entrance, and you start to think that the old ghost must have been mistaken or confused after so many centuries. In the end, in frustration, you give up the search. Return to **213**.

Trudging through the desolate landscape, you are alone except for a solitary bird riding the warm thermals above the hills. After an hour, you hear the sound of hoofs in the distance behind you. Turning around, you can make out a cloud of dust approaching from the south-west. As its gets closer you can see that riding towards you on a gaunt, haggard steed is a tall, thin man wearing scraps of armour and carrying a battered wooden shield and a wooden lance. He is accompanied by a short, round man riding a mule. You cannot avoid these two peculiar characters, so you wait for them to come up to you.

'Halt, stranger!' the tall man hails you. He is wearing a dented helmet and is sporting a drooping grey moustache and a pointed beard; he also looks well on in years 'What are you doing in this region?' he asks, almost accusingly. You tell him that you are on a vital mission and that time is of the essence. *Test your Luck*. If you are Lucky, turn to **342**. If you are Unlucky, turn to **102**.

147

Where will you go now: towards the Temple of Sithera (turn to **92**) or to the village (turn to **197**)?

148

The door is not locked, and on the other side is a regularly cut passageway leading both to left and to right. The walls are covered with stylized carvings of figures, human and semi-human, worshipping demonic idols. You decide not to gaze for too long at some of the scenes, so you move on swiftly. Will you go to the left (turn to **180**) or to the right (turn to **63**)?

149

Many of the tombs have been broken open and looted, while others are no more than piles of rubble. More disturbingly, however, you notice that the majority of those charnel-houses broken into have also had their sarcophagi smashed open – and the bodies are hissing. You begin to feel very uneasy, wandering among the empty burial sites, and you decide to get away from here as quickly as possible.

It is then that you hear dreadful moaning as a chorus of dead voices announce their presence. Blocking your way back is a horde of shambling, bandaged horrors. Some still look quite human, while others have become decayed, mouldering, bandage-wrapped skeletons. Will you face the Mummies and try to force a way through their ranks (turn to **303**), or will you flee (turn to **238**)?

150

Lopar unrolls the Papyrus Scroll and scans the columns of picture script. 'Ah,' he says, 'do you know what you have here?' You shake your head. 'This is a copy of the hieroglyphic alphabet that was used, centuries ago, by the people of Djarat.' The Shaman explains to you how to translate the hieroglyphs into Allansian. If you ever come across any of this hieroglyphic script, you will be able to translate it by subtracting 20 from the number of the paragraph you are on at the time, then turning to the new paragraph number. Now return to **194**.

151

The amulet you are wearing protects you from the Evil Eye which the High Priestess is trying to use against you. Before she can try anything else, you run at the devious woman. Turn to **350**.

152

The sun is low in the sky by the time you begin your ascent. In this light, Spirit Rock takes on a deep red hue and the veins of crystal sparkle as they catch the sun's last rays. If you have a rope and grapple, turn to **333**. Otherwise, turn to **391**.

153

You have entered what appears to be a throne-room. An ornate golden chair, inlaid with precious stones, stands on a raised platform between two arches. Carved in the wall next to the left-hand arch is the figure of a cat-headed woman, and the exit to the right has that of a man with a savage beast's head. Propped beside the throne are the skeletal remains of two Djaratian guards, doubtless buried along with their king millennia ago. You are determined to press on, since you feel that you haven't much further to go. Will you leave the throne-room via the right-hand archway (turn to **23**) or the left-hand one (turn to **260**)?

154

Making your way onwards through the tomb, you come to another junction. Will you veer off and follow the new passage that leads to the right (turn to **213**), or will you stick to this corridor (turn to **190**)?

155

Extracted from the White Lotus flower, this oil is clear and sweet-smelling, and is non-combustible. There is also not very much of it. Now return to **15**.

156

You have chosen badly. By moving Black Three you free White Four, which rapidly reaches the other end of the board. You have lost. Turn to **322**.

157

You press the next symbol and then the third. You can hear a grinding of stone on stone and wait for the door to open. Turn to **104**.

158

As you recover from the latest test of your mettle, you begin to itch all over and, looking at your hands, you can see scales forming on your skin! This mutation must be an effect of the poison on the Caarth's weapons! The irritation gradually dies down and, as you will no doubt soon discover, your affliction may have its advantages. If you ever suffer damage from edged weapons, such as swords or daggers, roll one dice; on a roll of 5 or 6, you may reduce that damage by 1 point, thanks to the hard scales covering your body. Turn to **231**.

159

Taking the sphere in your hands, you suffer no ill-effects. You sense that you can see something inside it, so you rub its surface to see if you can uncover anything. Suddenly you feel dizzy and disorientated. Your vision swims and the room spins round you until you are no longer sure that you are still in the same place. You close your eyes to try to stop the whirling and then, feeling steadier, open them again. Turn to **347**.

160

Mummies cannot move quickly because of their constricting bandages, so will you run at them with your sword drawn (turn to **51**) or, if you can, will you use something else against them first (turn to **103**)?

161

'I am sorry, but I cannot give you what you desire,' says the dog-headed Shaman. 'Now lie down beside this fire and let sleep take you.' Turn to **76**.

162

You are at a crossroads in the tunnels. Will you go left (turn to **195**), right (turn to **287**) or straight on (turn to **100**)?

163

The mummified animals stalk, prowl and slither towards you. In the confines of the corridor only two can attack you at the same time. (Any you have already destroyed come from the top of the list.)

	SKILL	STAMINA
JACKAL MUMMY	5	5
TIGER MUMMY	8	8
COBRA MUMMY	6	4

If you win but the cobra bit you at all, add 1 to your POISON score. Setting fire to the mummies with your light, they are turned to ashes in a few seconds; turn to **147**.

164

After days of wandering through the dust and heat of the desert hills, it makes a pleasant change to walk across a carpet of foliage between the trees at the edge of the pool. The cool waters of the oasis look even more tempting and refreshing now. Do you want to pause to drink here (turn to **187**), or will you leave the lush watering-hole to explore the temple ruins straight away (turn to **346**)?

165

When you push your weight against it, the stone door opens with ease into a set of store-rooms. Several recessed pantries lead off from a main corridor which is decorated with paintings of servants bearing offerings. Inside the alcoves are all kinds of food offerings, from loaves of bread and pitchers of wine, to dried meat and stuffed figs. After several thousand years, most of the food left for Akharis to consume in the afterlife has spoiled. However, if you want to spend some time searching, you could probably find some items that, preserved by the dry air of the tomb, are still edible. If you want to look for provisions, turn to **210**. Otherwise there is nothing else here, so you leave and follow the other passage (turn to **12**).

166

The process of removing the rocks from the blocked entrance is very tiring as well as time-consuming. Deduct 1 point from your STAMINA then roll one dice. If you roll an odd number, turn to **227**. If the number rolled is even, turn to **319**.

167

'What help do you require?' the man asks. Will you ask whether he can aid you in any way on your quest (turn to **339**) or ask him what he knows of the Shaman (turn to **389**)?

168

Shaking the rattle, you advance on the Mummy — who merely punches you in the stomach, causing you to drop the charm. Deduct 2 points from your STAMINA and turn to **215**.

169

Your feet touch the tunnel floor and you are safely over the chasm. Having rested for a minute, you set off again, until you come to a junction. Will you now go to the left (turn to **40**) or to the right (turn to **9**)?

170

Having constructed your fire, you settle down to sleep. *Test your Luck*. If you are Lucky, the night passes peacefully (restore 2 STAMINA points) and in the morning, having consulted Jerran's map once more, you head north towards the temple (turn to **5**). If you are Unlucky, turn to **375**.

171

After all you have had to face, your muscles are just too weak to achieve the mighty task you need them for. As the burial chamber fills with sand, you have to abandon your attempt and consign yourself to death. In minutes the chamber is full and your adventure is over.

172

Before you can throw yourself out of the way, the mud-ball rolls into you, knocking you to the ground. Several of the stones embedded in it gash your arms and legs (deduct 2 points from your STAMINA). As you struggle to stand up, the beetle attacks.

GIANT SCARAB BEETLE   SKILL 7   STAMINA 8

For the first Attack Round of this battle reduce your Attack Strength by 1 point as you are still getting to your feet. If you defeat the overgrown insect, turn to **351**.

173

You take a swig from the jar and swallow quickly. You immediately double up in pain as a terrible burning sensation assails your stomach. The plants the pungent syrup is made from are toxic (deduct 4 points from your STAMINA and add 2 to your POISON score). Now do you want to try rubbing some of the syrup on your body instead (turn to **219**) or drinking some of the sweet-smelling liquid (turn to **82**), or will you leave the embalming chambers (turn to **379**)?

174

Scrambling down from the safety of the rocky ledge, you walk slowly towards the beast. Hearing your footsteps, the Dracon turns its head in your direction and lets out a terrifying roar. You notice that, with the creature's struggling, the stakes holding the net down are coming loose. Do you want to:

Show the beast you mean it no harm and keep walking towards it?	Turn to **196**
Draw your sword and prepare to defend yourself?	Turn to **382**
Make a run for it while you still can?	Turn to **273**

175

'Very well,' the Sphinx intones. 'Here is your first question. Who designed and built the tomb of the evil one whom you seek?' If you know the name that is the answer to the Sphinx's question, convert it into a number using the code A = 1, B = 2, C = 3 and so on; then turn to the paragraph with the same number. If you do not know the name, turn to **262**.

176

Before you can reach the Mummies, a cold shiver passes over you. The statue of Sithera is glowering down at you malevolently. Suddenly, a cultist leaps into your path wielding a huge, curved blade! You must fight him.

ELITE CULTIST   SKILL 10   STAMINA 8

If the battle lasts more than six Attack Rounds, more cultists surround you; turn to **338**. If the battle lasts six rounds or fewer, and you win, turn to **138**.

177

Opening the darkwood door, you enter a square room, on the far side of which an archway leads into a second, darkened chamber from which you can hear a hissing noise and the slithering of scaly bodies.

However, before you will be able to reach that chamber you will have to defeat the guardians of this outer one. Dressed in faded Djaratian robes, two horrifying figures are advancing towards you. In the flickering light you can make out their skeletal human bodies, and you recoil at the sight of their serpent heads, still covered in patches of snake-skin, and their glowing red eyes. If you would rather slam the door shut again and escape from here immediately, turn to **54**; otherwise, you will have to fight Sithera's minions at the same time as they attack with taloned hands.

	SKILL	STAMINA
First DEMONIC SERVANT	8	7
Second DEMONIC SERVANT	7	7

If you succeed in winning two consecutive Attack Rounds against either of these hellspawn, the spell animating its body will be broken and it will collapse into a pile of bones. If you defeat the Demonic Servants, turn to **140**.

178

The sun sets over the western horizon and you settle down to rest between some rocks. The night is warm and you are soon fast asleep . . .

You wake up with a start, hearing the snuffling sound made by some large creature near by. You have just unsheathed your sword when the beast comes into view between the boulders. In the moonlight the creature looks like a cross between a bear and an ape, but it is larger than either. Smelling you, the Nandibear turns to face you and lets out a blood-curdling howl. It has decided that tonight it will feast on its favourite food – human brains!

NANDIBEAR   SKILL 9   STAMINA 11

If you manage to kill this ferocious monster, turn to **244**.

179

There are riches here beyond your wildest dreams! Mesmerized by the treasure hoard before you, you are only dimly aware of a rushing sound coming from the main chamber. At last you look around – and see with horror that the burial chamber is filling with sand, pouring down from holes in the ceiling. It is already knee deep as you wade back towards the door, where you find that it has closed again and that there is no handle on this side! In a matter of minutes the room will be completely filled with the sands of the desert above, burying you alive. Greed has proved to be your downfall!

180

The passage continues for quite a way without changing direction. At last you come to a black-painted door in the right-hand wall of the passage; a silver handle protrudes from it. Do you want to try to open this door (turn to **228**) or walk further along the passage (turn to **296**)?

181

If you have some Firepowder or a Yokka Egg, you can use either of them to distract the Cyclops; *Test your Skill* if you do this and, if you are successful, reduce its STAMINA score by the appropriate amount before fighting it (turn to **248**). If you do not have any such special items, you will have to be satisfied with throwing rocks at the beast. *Test your Skill*. If you are successful, roll one dice. If you roll a 6, turn to **199**; if you roll any other number, deduct 2 points from the Cyclops' STAMINA before fighting it; turn to **248**. Even if you fail, you still attract the monster's attention, even though you do not wound it; turn to **248**.

182

Eventually you reach a T-junction. Will you now go to the left (turn to **48**) or to the right (turn to **124**)?

183

There can be no doubt that the Golem was an emissary of the Cult of the Cobra, sent to stop you reaching the tomb. As the day grows hotter, you redouble your efforts and force yourself onwards, determined to thwart the evil sect's plans. At last you find yourself gazing over the top of a great rift in the hills. At the bottom of the steep-sided, sand-blown valley you can clearly see a dark rectangular opening in the side of a cliff, surrounded by large, carefully cut blocks of stone bearing carved reliefs which are unmistakably Djaratian. You have found the Tomb of Akharis! However, you may still not be able to enter safely, since from your vantage-point you can see two giant, four-legged lizards standing close to the entrance. Both are saddled and harnessed, but there is no sign of whoever or whatever has ridden them here. Do you want to approach the tomb immediately (turn to **276**) or will you wait to see whether any further developments ensue (turn to **119**)?

184

You manage to trap White Four securely, but White Two is left unchallenged and in three moves the game is all over: Nemset has won. Turn to **322**.

185

Yelling, you run at the leader of the cultists. At the last moment he deftly sidesteps out of your way, and you end up sprawling in the dirt. *Test your Luck*. If you are Lucky, turn to **363**. If you are Unlucky, turn to **55**.

186

Standing on the plinth, clear of the snakes, you study the box and find that it has a simple, hinged lid. It is only after you have opened the iron casket that you discover a problem: lying in the bottom of the box is a long, rolled-up papyrus scroll and crawling all around and over it are several deadly scorpions, each as big as a man's hand. If you want to take the scroll, *Test your Skill*. If you are successful, you lift it out safely; turn to **200**. If you fail, you disturb the scorpions and have to endure their stings! Roll one dice and divide the result by two (rounding fractions up), then add this number to your POISON score; turn to **200**. Alternatively, you may decide against retrieving the scroll and so attempt to leave the room; turn to **111**.

187

Kneeling down at the water's edge, you cup your hands together and, having dipped them in the pool, gulp down a great mouthful. Almost instantly your stomach is seized by a terrible burning pain. The water of the oasis is poisoned! You writhe around in agony for several minutes before the acute pain passes, but you are left feeling weak and nauseous (deduct 4 points from your STAMINA and add 2 to your POISON score). Once you feel able to continue again, you leave the treacherous oasis to explore the ruined remains of the temple. Turn to **346**.

188

You run full pelt at one of the slabs of rock and hit it with a painful crack, dislocating your shoulder! Doubled up in agony, you can do nothing to halt the slow but steady descent of the roof. Your adventure ends here.

189

You have not gone much further when suddenly a bizarre creature appears over the crest of a sand-dune in front of you. Its head and torso are human, but from the waist down its lower body and legs are those of a giant ant! The Xoroa, for that is what you are now facing, stands two metres tall and is coloured a deep reddish brown all over. The creature's eyes are silver and, instead of outer ears, two flexible, ant-like feelers extend forward from the top of its head. This Xoroa Warrior has been patrolling the area round its colony and it makes angry clicking sounds at your intrusion. Armed with a short spear, the guard attacks instantly.

XOROA WARRIOR   SKILL 10   STAMINA 11

If you win, turn to **331**.

190

The further you progress, the more cracks and fissures you notice covering the floor of the tunnel. Just as you are considering turning back, the tunnel floor gives way and, yelling, you fall through utter darkness for several seconds. Your cry is cut short by the shock of hitting water. Surfacing, you allow your body to be carried along by the fast-moving current of a subterranean river. Turn to **280**.

191

Your sword drawn, you run into the room uttering a shout. At the last instant, the cultist turns and prepares to defend himself with the staff he is carrying.

CULTIST   SKILL 7   STAMINA 7

If you win, a swift search of the cultist's clothes reveals nothing of use to you except two meals' worth of provisions (add these to your *Adventure Sheet*). Still no wiser as to the cultist's actions, you search the chamber but discover nothing. All you can do now is continue along the tunnel; eventually it turns right again, bringing you to the top of another flight of stone steps that lead still deeper into the tomb. You have no choice but to descend; turn to **216**.

192

The talisman starts to feel hot. Holding it up by its chain, you see that the sun is glowing brightly. There is a sudden flash, then a blazing beam of light shoots from the amulet into the undead horde with devastating effect. Several of the Mummies immediately burst into flames as their bone-dry wrappings ignite under the heat of the beam. Roll one dice and add 2. Make a note that this is the number of Mummies you have already destroyed. The talisman's power is expended, but Akharis's servants have already suffered the wrath of the sun god! Now will you attack the remaining undead with fire (turn to **18**) or your sword (turn to **51**)?

193

Catching you off guard, the serpent evades your feeble blows and strikes swiftly. In an instant its mouth has closed round you and the monster swallows you whole! Trapped inside its stomach, you quickly suffocate before its powerful digestive acids begin their work.

194
The Shaman can tell you more about an object only if you have a number associated with it. If you do have such an item, multiply the appropriate number by thirty, then turn to the paragraph whose number is the same as the total. After you have discovered more about your object, you will be returned to this paragraph. When you have finished showing Lopar your items, he says to you, 'Now lie down beside this fire and let sleep take you.' Turn to 76.

195
The only sound in the tunnels is the gentle lapping of the water against the walls. Rounding a corner, you come to a large intersection. Which way will you go now?

First left?	Turn to 301
Second left?	Turn to 234
First right?	Turn to 69
Second right?	Turn to 217
Straight ahead?	Turn to 142

196
Raising your hands in a gesture of peace, you move closer to the Dracon, telling it that you mean it no harm. You are somewhat surprised when the beast snarls in reply, 'Well, get this infernal net off me then!'

Will you do as the creature demands (turn to **21**) or leave it bound (turn to **382**)?

197

At present you are wandering through the deserted streets of a Djaratian workmen's village where the people who laboured to build the Necropolis once lived. Their basic dwellings are in ruins now and there is nothing of use to you here. However, as you are returning to the central avenue through the City of the Dead you come upon a craftsman's workshop, still almost intact. Looking inside, you notice an iron ring attached to a flagstone in the middle of the room. If you want to try to lift the flagstone, turn to **67**. Alternatively, you can leave the workmen's village and explore the low stone buildings, if you haven't already done so (turn to **56**), or make for the Temple of Sithera (turn to **92**).

198

The inscription reads: *Twice upon the door to knock, thrice upon the door unlock.* If you know how many times you must knock upon the door, turn to the paragraph with the same number. If you do not, you will have to press on further into the tomb, turn to **374**.

199

Unbelievably, your rock hits the Cyclops on its temple in just the right place to kill it outright! Regain 1 LUCK point. Turn to **52**.

200

Unrolling part of the scroll, you see that it is covered in picture-writing and illustrations in the Djaratian style. Scanning the first few columns of hieroglyphs, and utilizing your growing knowledge of the ancient Djaratian language, you translate them to discover their meaning. It appears that the scroll you have in your hands is an ancient Djaratian 'Book of the Dead', a guide to the journey through the underworld containing spells to aid dead people making the journey and information such as the fact that they must face thirteen hazards on their journey. This could prove very useful. Rolling up the scroll again, you put it in your backpack. Turn to **111**.

201

Your sixth sense screaming danger, you throw yourself forward just as the floor gives way beneath you. You land heavily just on the far side of the pit-trap, winded but alive. The bottom of the deep, sheer-sided pit is filled with cruelly pointed metal spikes! You had a close escape indeed! You continue on your way extremely cautiously. The passage soon turns to the right and, following it, you come upon an archway, surrounded by carvings, in the left-hand wall. If you followed a cultist into the tomb, turn to **43**. If you did not, turn to **71**.

202

Hearing a clicking sound, you look along the length of the room. At its far end, standing in front of a grand set of double doors, are two terrifying creatures. They appear to be a cross between humans and gigantic scorpions, with the heads and torsos of men but the bodies and deadly stings of desert arachnids. Carrying polearms, these are the demonic Accursed, once human but now servants of the Demon Prince. If you are to gain access to the third level of the tomb, you will have to vanquish them in battle. Because of their great size, fight the Accursed one at a time.

	SKILL	STAMINA
First ACCURSED	10	10
Second ACCURSED	9	11

If either of the Accursed wins an Attack Round, roll one dice. On a roll of 5 or 6, instead of hitting you with their polearms, they strike you with their stings (add 1 to your POISON score as well as losing 2 points from your STAMINA). If you overcome the demonic guards, turn to 153.

203

Evading the Mummy's flailing arms, you grab the death-mask and pull it from Akharis's head, flinging it to the ground. At once the Mummy howls with pain and its movement seems to become slower. Your action has cost Akharis 1 SKILL point and 2 STAMINA points of damage (remember to make a note of the number of points of damage Akharis has already suffered). You now have no choice but to fight the Mummy. Turn to **97**.

204

You find yourself walking along a rectangular passage-way cut into the rock of the cliff. Daylight entering from outside illuminates the tunnel for only a short way – beyond that there is nothing but darkness. If you have a permanent light-source, say a lantern, torch or lamp, turn to **307**. If you have no means to light your way, turn to **233**.

205

This is a foolish move which leaves the way clear for White Four. Nemset wins the game in just two moves. Turn to **322**.

206

Your reflexes are not quick enough. Helplessly you plunge into the pit, the bottom of which is filled with bubbling acid. No one escapes from the Venom of the Cobra!

207

You have almost reached the cave entrance when you fall. There is no way you could survive a fall from such a height. When you hit the ground, your body is smashed to pieces on the boulders at the foot of Spirit Rock. Your adventure is over.

208

Keeping out of sight of the guards, you creep round the side of the pyramid and soon discover an alternative way into the temple. There is a small hole, halfway up the side of the pyramid several metres above you. You could easily scramble up to it – but it could be a trap. Do you want to risk it and climb up to the hole (turn to **77**), or will you use the main entrance after all (turn to **132**)?

209

The small pyramid has been carved out of a piece of quartz crystal; it refracts the light from the sun inside it into a myriad colours. Now return to **15**.

210

Your search is quite fruitful and you manage to accumulate enough food for 4 meals (add these to your *Adventure Sheet*). Preparing to leave the offerings chambers, you turn back towards the stone door. With a cracking sound, fragments of plaster start flaking off one of the wall-paintings. You watch, startled, as a life-size figure from the mural begins to emerge from the wall, assuming a three-dimensional form as it does so. The Djaratians believed that figures of servants painted in the tombs would magically come to life to serve the dead king. This is exactly what is happening now as the food store's guardian prepares to deal with a thief – you!

TOMB GUARDIAN   SKILL 7   STAMINA 6

If you kill the servant, at your final blow the guardian crumbles into a heap of plaster-dust, allowing you to leave. Turn to **12**.

211

You try to leap out of the way but the lance strikes you in the middle of your chest, pushing you to the ground (deduct 3 points from your STAMINA). Unsheathing his rusted weapon, the man bears down on you, shouting, 'Die, Demon! You cannot prevail against the honour of Don Huan Fernandez, Knight of Vastille!' For the first Attack Round, reduce your Attack Strength by 1 point because you are lying on the ground.

FERNANDEZ   SKILL 7   STAMINA 7

If you reduce your opponent's STAMINA score to 3 points or less, turn immediately to **253**.

212

Because you have the element of surprise, the cultist is prevented from using any trickery against you, and you gain an unopposed strike. Then the cultist snarls and turns on you.

CULTIST   SKILL 6   STAMINA 5

If you win, turn to **36**.

213

Trudging through the deathly stillness of the tomb, you wonder what other surprises and horrors await you before your quest comes to an end. The tunnel turns right and you continue to walk along it for several metres. Turn to **254**.

214

As your opponent falls, so does Jerran's. Before you can stop him, the third cultist turns tail and flees towards the markets. What will you do now? Will you pursue the cultist and try to stop him before he can warn the rest of the sect (turn to **394**), leave Rimon immediately, with the intention of heading the cultist off on the way to the tomb (turn to **242**), or ignore the cultist and visit the markets to prepare for your quest (turn to **112**)?

215

You now have only three options open to you, since Akharis is upon you. You can either attack him with your sword (turn to **97**), try to remove his death-mask (turn to **293**) or try to destroy the sarcophagus (turn to **257**).

216

As you descend the steps you are amazed at the amount of heat, transmitted through the sand and rock of the desert above, in the tomb. Through your constant exertions, beads of sweat start to break out on your skin. The staircase leads into a low-ceilinged, square chamber, on the far side of which is a fine wooden door with gilded handles.

However, resting against the wall to the left of the door is a grotesque, mouldering, human skeleton, still wrapped in rotting clothes. The air round the corpse is heavy with disease and decay, and sunk deep in their sockets are two vacant, sickly yellow eyes. Cautiously you step towards the door and immediately the skeleton comes to life and lurches jerkily towards you, its claws raised. You are going to have to fight the foul Decayer! Will you use your sword (turn to **258**) or some other weapon (turn to **135**)?

217

All the tunnels look very much alike. Coming to a junction, will you now take the first to the left (turn to **301**) or the second to the left (turn to **182**), or turn to the right (turn to **272**)?

218

You have strayed inside the boundary of the land round a Xoroa colony which the two Warriors you are now facing have been guarding. You must fight the ant-men at the same time.

	SKILL	STAMINA
First XOROA WARRIOR	10	11
Second XOROA WARRIOR	10	10

If you manage to defeat both of them, turn to **331**.

219

The syrup is used by embalmers to toughen and preserve the body as part of the mummification process. Rubbing it on your skin toughens it so that from now on you may reduce any external physical injuries you may suffer, say in battle, by 1 STAMINA point. However, this toughening makes your skin less flexible and so hampers movement (reduce both your current and *Initial* SKILL by 2). Now will you:

Drink some of the syrup?	Turn to **173**
Drink from the other jar?	Turn to **82**
Leave this place?	Turn to **379**

220

Putting the horn to your lips, you blow hard. A resonating blast echoes across the hills but does nothing to stop the Golem's advance. A gritty fist strikes you in the face (deduct 2 points from your STAMINA). Swiftly you draw your sword, ready to retaliate. Turn to **143**.

221

Just in case the undead Vizier's insane loyalty should bring him back to life once more, you set fire to his corpse. Having done so, you do not delay in leaving the treasure chamber, but on your way out you grab a handful of gems, worth between 3 and 8 Gold Pieces (roll one dice and add 2 to the number rolled) and a Bronze Rattle – a sacred device used in religious ceremonies. Now turn to **105**.

222

Desperately you hack at the swarm with your sword, trying to prevent the wasps from stinging you. Fight the insects as if they were one opponent.

SWARM   SKILL 9   STAMINA 7

Because the swarm is made up of many creatures, it will be difficult to injure, so for the duration of this battle you must reduce your Attack Strength by 1 point. If the swarm wins an Attack Round, deduct 2 points from your STAMINA and add 1 to your POISON score. If you win, turn to **302**.

223

'So, you managed to retrieve the Serpent's Eye from the tomb,' the priestess says with a voice like velvet. 'In that case, obey my will. Kneel!' You are unable to resist. The evil artefact round your neck makes you susceptible to the will of the Demon Prince's minions. You remain motionless as the life-force is drawn from your body so that Akharis may live again.

224

There is nothing remarkable about the key, and Cranno tells you he has never found a lock that it fits. Return to **339**.

225

Time will wait no longer. As you watch, the ghost of Rhehotep fades. 'May the good gods of Djarat go with you, brave adventurer . . .' is the last thing you hear him say before his spirit departs this world at last. Turn to 154.

226

Dusk falls and still you have not sighted the temple. Here, on the fringes of the Desert of Skulls, the nights are as freezing as the days are scorching. If you have a Yokka Egg, turn to 83. Otherwise, do you want to build a fire to keep you warm, assuming you have some means of lighting one (turn to 170), or would you rather not risk attracting the attentions of any nocturnal hunters (turn to 31)?

227

As you clear away the rubble, you are interrupted in your labours by the arrival of one of the tomb's wandering guards. With lifeless, rotting flesh, long dank hair and tatters of Djaratian garments clinging to its decaying flesh, the Tomb Stalker stumbles towards you, moaning. If you do not want to fight the deathly guard, you can stop clearing the passageway and run back along the tunnel, following it past the cedar-wood doors (turn to 254). Otherwise, you will have to fight.

TOMB STALKER   SKILL 8   STAMINA 6

If the Tomb Stalker wins two consecutive Attack Rounds, it will grab your neck in its powerful hands and strangle you, causing damage equal to the roll of one dice! Each Attack Round after this, you must strike successfully to free yourself from its grip or take the same extra damage again. If you overcome the undead guard, turn to **319**.

228

The door opens into an antechamber which is decorated with painted reliefs of the Djaratians at war with various nations and desert tribes. Beyond this room, through an archway, is another, smaller one. In the centre of this second room stands a plain alabaster pedestal on which, glinting in the light you are carrying, you see a small figurine of a cat made from jet. As you consider taking this treasure, you become aware of the two life-size statues of men, armed with spears, standing one either side of the archway. Do you want to enter the inner chamber and take the cat (turn to **251**) or will you leave this room and return to the passage outside (turn to **296**)?

229

Entering the passageway, there is a sudden drop in temperature and you cannot help feeling that your light does not penetrate the darkness as well as it should. Without warning, a huge claw sinks into your back, tearing your flesh to the bone. Screaming in pain, you stare, horrified, as a great ball of fire comes hurtling down the corridor and engulfs you. From amid the flames, a spear-wielding corpse thrusts its weapon between your ribs, and all around cruel faces laugh at your distress. Can this really be happening? *Test your Skill.* If you succeed, turn to **70**. If you fail, turn to **32**.

230

You press the vulture symbol next and then the snake. There is a moment of tense anticipation as you wonder whether you have made the right choice, then the wall swings open. Stepping through the secret door, you find yourself in a short corridor which ends after only ten metres at a bizarre portal carved to resemble a gaping serpent's mouth. Between the fangs, pin-pricks of silver light swirl within a black void. There is no sign of the cultist, and the portal is the only way forward, so will you enter it (turn to **347**) or retrace your steps to the original tunnel, which turns right and leads you deeper into the tomb down a flight of steps (turn to **216**)?

231

As you search the Snakemen's bodies, you wonder what they are doing in the tomb. The Giant Lizards you encountered must have been their mounts. It is likely that the Caarth were investigating goings-on here because of the proximity to their lands and the connection with the Demon Prince, Sith, whom they worship. These two can only have been scouts from a larger party, as they are carrying nothing of use to you in terms of provisions or treasure.

Leaving the dead Caarth, you make your way to the far side of the pillared hall and leave through an archway, which is the only exit. You enter another short passage which ends at a T-junction. Both routes look exactly the same, so far as you can see by your light, so will you take the left- (turn to 396) or the right-hand tunnel (turn to 75)?

232

In the alcove is a crystal orb, resting on a golden stand, an alabaster bowl containing brightly coloured powders, and a flask, fashioned in the form of a viper, containing some black liquid. What will you try to use to aid your escape?

The crystal orb?	Turn to 58
The coloured powders?	Turn to 126
The viper's venom?	Turn to 297

233

You proceed carefully along the tunnel into the all-enveloping blackness. Slowly edging forward, you find yourself at the top of a flight of steps and begin to make your way down. Totally blind in the darkness, you do not see the missing steps and, losing your footing, fall the rest of the way down the steep, very long staircase. Lying at the bottom of the steps, stunned, you are only dimly aware of the sound of footsteps and a sibiliant hissing before a poisoned blade is plunged into your heart. You perish horribly in the darkness. Your adventure is over.

234

You pass under a section of roof covered with thick slime and, as you do so, some drips on to you. Unfortunately the vile gunk is acidic (deduct 2 points from your STAMINA). Now where will you go?

Left, then left again?	Turn to 182
Left, then straight on?	Turn to 195
Straight on?	Turn to 369

235

Crouching low against the top of the cliffs, you encounter no hostile denizens of these parts and, once past the gorge, you follow a stony track down towards the lower ground and rejoin your original path. Turn to 90.

236

While you battle on, the other Mummies slowly surround you and grab you with their decaying hands. Unable to move, you are totally helpless as the High Priestess casts her spell, draining your life-force to resurrect Akharis. Your adventure is over.

237

Throwing aside his mask, the man runs down the steps from the platform and falls to his knees beside the prone body of his dead pet, tears streaming down his face. Then he turns to you and, between great sobs, manages to splutter, 'I'm sorry. Oh please have mercy. I don't mean anyone any harm; I just like to be left in peace.' Seeing the man in such a state, you are filled with remorse and leave the ruined theatre before you cause Cranno any more grief. Turn to **8**.

238

You turn tail and run into the labyrinthine depths of the tomb district. Rounding a corner, you almost run straight into another group of Mummies, then a third group emerges from a side-street. Surrounded, you do your best to fend off the lumbering undead but, even with fire as a weapon, you are eventually overcome by the sheer force of their numbers. Your adventure is over.

239

You have not travelled far along the passage when you come to a junction: another low corridor leads away to the left. Do you want to follow this new tunnel (turn to **305**) or would you prefer to stick to your present route (turn to **254**)?

240

While you are lighting the torch, the wasps can sting you unopposed (deduct 2 points from your STAMINA and add 1 to your POISON score). However, wielding the blazing torch, you will be able to harm the swarm more effectively.

SWARM   SKILL 9   STAMINA 7

Because you are using an unusual weapon, you must reduce your Attack Strength by 1 point for the duration of this battle. If the swarm wins an Attack Round, as well as losing 2 STAMINA points you must add 1 to your POISON score. If you overcome the swarm, turn to 302.

241

If you are wearing a Sun Talisman, multiply the number of light rays projecting from it by eight, then turn to the paragraph with the same number as the total. Anything else you may have has no effect on these undead; so will you fight them with fire (turn to 18) or with your sword (turn to 51)?

242

Leaving Rimon, Jerran Farr and yourself set out round the steep Uron Heights, before turning north. As you walk, Jerran shows you a crude map of the area round the southern edge of the Desert of Skulls and points to a sketch of an oasis next to a temple. 'I was able to get the location of the temple from the explorer before he died, but not that of the tomb,' says Jerran, 'but if we can find the temple, we should find the inscription that reveals the whereabouts of the tomb. I have also heard rumours of a Shaman who lives in the rocky hills to the east, at a place called Spirit Rock. If we could find him, he may be able to help us in our quest. However, we'll leave the choosing of the way until it becomes necessary.'

After two days of walking (during which time you must eat 2 meals or lose 2 STAMINA points for each meal missed) you reach the site of Jerran's camp. Here he has hidden a tent and bed-rolls, so at dusk you settle down for a night under canvas. You are woken several hours later by an ominous clacking sound coming from somewhere close to the tent. There is a sudden scuttling noise, then you hear Jerran cry out. In an instant you are outside the tent. In the moonlight you see the archaeologist struggling in the grip of a huge pincer belonging to a three-metre-long monstrosity covered in shiny black armour. The Giant Scorpion's sting rears up over its back, as large as a man's head. As you watch, the deadly sting of the overgrown arachnid lashes forward and strikes Jerran in the chest and the man stops struggling at once. You run at the scorpion and strike its claw. Releasing its grip on Jerran's body, the grotesque creature turns to attack you.

GIANT SCORPION   SKILL 8   STAMINA 10

Each claw can attack independently, so conduct this fight as if you were up against two opponents, each with a SKILL of 10. If at any time the Scorpion's Attack Strength is 22, turn at once to **137**. If you win, turn to **345**.

243

It is a close-run thing, but you just beat Nemset to the end of the board. You have won! 'I congratulate you, adventurer,' Nemset says graciously. 'For your success you deserve a prize.' The ghost directs you to a golden casket inside the tomb. Opening it, you find an amulet on a golden chain, representing the sun, with twenty-four stylized rays of light projecting from it. There is also a small, decorative glass bottle, full of water, etched with the Djaratian symbol for life. 'Take the Sun Talisman and the Waters of Life,' says the princess, 'and may they help you thwart the evil one.' If you ever want to drink the Waters of Life (but not when you are in the middle of a combat), make a note of the paragraph you are reading at the time, then turn to **355**. For now, add your new possessions to your *Adventure Sheet*, then turn to **322**.

244

The rest of the night passes without incident, and in the morning you are able to inspect the body of the

Nandibear. The creature still lies where it fell and you can make out its tracks among the rocks. Its lair cannot be far away, and you wonder what treasures could be hidden there. If you want to follow the Nandibear's tracks in the hope of finding its lair, turn to **117**. If you would rather not make this diversion from your journey, turn to **337**.

245

Unfurling the scroll, you scan the columns of hieroglyphs for a spell to help you. As you do so, Akharis grabs you and hurls you to the floor (deduct 4 points from your STAMINA). Dropping the scroll, you prepare to fight; turn to **215**.

246

You side-step swiftly so that the mud-ball rolls past you harmlessly. Angrily, the beetle scuttles forward to attack.

GIANT SCARAB BEETLE   SKILL 7   STAMINA 8

If you overcome the overgrown insect, turn to **351**.

247

Proceeding along the tunnel, you are startled to hear the sound of rushing water in the distance. The noise increases in volume until you come to the edge of a precipice. Shining your light into the darkness, you see that the crevasse is several metres wide and that the tunnel continues on the other side. Your illumination also picks out the craggy sides of the chasm but does not reach as far as the water you can hear roaring below. Somehow you will either have to get across to the other side of the crevasse or risk jumping into the underground river. Will you:

Attempt to jump across the chasm?	Turn to **292**
Use a rope and grapple, if you have one, to swing across?	Turn to **271**
Jump into the river?	Turn to **386**

248

Yelling, you charge at the Cyclops and, before it can react, sink your blade into its leg. Bellowing with pain and rage, the monster forgets Fernandez and turns all its fury on you.

CYCLOPS   SKILL 10   STAMINA 10

If you win, turn to **52**.

249

The tunnel comes to an end in a flooded room. Manacled to a wall is a human skeleton and hanging from its neck is an obsidian pendant, which you may take if you wish. Leaving the room, you return to the intersection. Will you take the first to the right (turn to **195**), the second to the right (turn to **272**), the third to the right (turn to **182**), the first to the left (turn to **69**), the second to the left (turn to **301**) or go straight ahead (turn to **142**)?

250

You trudge on through the heat of the day, further into the rugged hills. The only vegetation that grows in this hot region is the occasional scrubby bush and fleshy, green, thick-stemmed succulent covered in spines. You notice one of these plants growing close to the track you are following. Some species are very nutritious, but you do not know if this is such a one. Do you want to cut yourself a piece of the plant to eat (turn to **110**) or will you continue on your way (turn to **11**)?

251

You pass through the archway between the statues unhindered and lift the jet figurine from the pedestal without triggering any lethal device. It is only when you approach the archway again that the nature of the trap here becomes clear. Creaking, the two statues move from their sentry-posts of centuries and advance towards the tomb robber who would steal the treasure they guard. Standing in the archway, you may fight the statues one at a time.

	SKILL	STAMINA
First STATUE	8	8
Second STATUE	8	9

If you win, the second statue shatters as you lay your final blow. Stowing the Jet Cat in your backpack, you leave the room and continue along the passageway in search of further treasures. Turn to **296**.

Lying at the bottom of the sarcophagus, among a few scraps of stained, torn bandages, is an amulet in the form of a stylized eye (you may take it if you wish). So where can Akharis's body be? The Cult of the Cobra must have moved it from the tomb and taken it elsewhere. Having braved the tomb's dark depths, you are overwhelmed with dejection, fearing that your perilous journey may have been a complete waste of time! You are roused from your state of self-pity by a rushing sound. Looking up, you see in horror that the burial chamber is filling with sand which is pouring down from holes in the ceiling. The door slams shut and there is no handle on the inside! The last trap has been sprung and, if you cannot find a way out soon, you are going to be buried alive. *Test your Skill.* If you succeed, turn to **109**. If you fail, turn to **42**.

253

'Retreat! Retreat!' the old man yells, acknowledging your superior swordsmanship and breaking off his attack. Pulling on his steed's reins, Fernandez gallops away north-eastwards into the hills, followed by Gordo on his mule. Bewildered by the old man's irrational actions, you watch as the two figures dwindle into the distance before continuing your journey on foot. Turn to **24**.

254

Following the passage, you find yourself in a small square room with a door in each of its four walls. As you stand in the middle of the room, considering which way to go next, there is a loud grating sound and four great slabs of stone drop down, blocking all the exits! You run over to one blocked doorway and hammer on it with your fist. As if things were not bad enough already, now you hear a deep rumbling sound and the roof of the chamber begins to descend as great metal spikes emerge from holes cut into it. You were not quick enough in leaving this room, so now you will die by the Fangs of Sithera! What are you going to do to prevent such a grisly fate? Will you:

Ram one of the doors?	Turn to **188**
Try to jam the descending ceiling?	Turn to **66**
Search for a release mechanism?	Turn to **362**

255

As soon as you touch the statue, a magical transformation takes place and the golden image grows until it is two and a half metres tall. The huge crocodile-head looks down at you then raises a great golden fist, ready to beat you into the ground. Do you have a Gold Piece or something else made of gold among your possessions? If you have, turn to **78**. If you haven't, turn to **275**.

256

Looking through the telescope, you are amazed by how close distant features appear. In the east, a single high pinnacle of rock juts up from among the hills into the sky. A massive boulder seems to be balanced on top of it and you can make out shining, swirling patterns on its surface. Surely this must be Spirit Rock! Turning to the north, your eye is caught by the reflection of the sun on water. Surrounding the oasis is a group of palm trees and next to it, lying in tumbled ruins, is the temple you seek. Turn to **235**.

257

To reach the sarcophagus, you will first have to get past Akharis himself. The foul Mummy reaches out for you with bandaged talons. (Remember to deduct any points of damage you have already inflicted on Akharis.)

AKHARIS   SKILL 13   STAMINA 25

As soon as you have fought four rounds of combat, you get past the lurching undead horror and run up the dais steps to the sarcophagus. But how will you destroy it? There are several large cracks across the coffin, but you feel sure that striking it with your sword will have little effect. If you have some Firepowder you could use, turn to 373. Otherwise, you decide to try to push the great stone coffin off the dais, hoping that the fall will break it. Roll four dice; if the total is greater than your STAMINA score, you are not strong enough to carry out such a herculean feat (turn to 97). If the total is less than or equal to your STAMINA score, you succeed in pushing the sarcophagus off the dais so that it hits the floor with devastating results (turn to 373).

258

Reeking of death and putrefaction, the undead Decayer advances towards you, fearless of your weapon.

DECAYER	SKILL 7	STAMINA 5

Unknown to you, while you were fighting you have been infected by the near-invisible, disease-ridden spores released by the Decayer (so, if you win, add 4 to your POISON score); turn to 148.

259

'Run for it!' you shout to Jerran, and the two of you charge the lone cultist behind you. Knocking him to the ground, the way along the street ahead is clear as far as the markets. Once among the crowds, you should be able to lose your pursuers easily. Suddenly you hear a humming sound as two throwing-stars fly from the cultists' hands and strike you and Jerran in the back (deduct 2 points from your STAMINA). You stumble to the ground and the cultists are upon you. Turn to **68**.

260

As you walk towards the left-hand exit, the guards' bones rise jerkily from their posts and advance towards you. They will reach the archway before you do, so, if you want to avoid clashing with the guards you could change direction and run through the other exit (turn to **229**). If you are intent on passing through this archway, you will have to fight.

	SKILL	STAMINA
First SKELETAL GUARD	8	6
Second SKELETAL GUARD	7	6

If you win, turn to **371**.

261

'You are no Demon,' he says, looking slightly bewildered. 'Perhaps that black-hearted scoundrel Zanmethees did not send you.' You assure Fernandez that he did not and, convinced at last, the old knight apologizes profusely for his previous behaviour. In order to make amends he offers you a purse containing 6 Gold Pieces. If you accept this gift, add the treasure to your *Adventure Sheet*. Now that the Cyclops is dead, the cowardly Gordo, Fernandez's manservant, emerges from his hiding place to tend his master's wounds; you waste no more time in returning to your original route towards the temple. Turn to **226**.

262

The Sphinx speaks again, but still you do not know what to say in reply. There is a tense moment of silence, then the great creature roars, bounding towards you across the hall. Bewildered, you unsheath your sword to defend yourself. Unfortunately, your earthly weapon has no effect against this agent of the gods of Djarat, whereas its terrible claws soon tear you apart. Your adventure is over.

263

The stone whistles past your head, missing it by just a few centimetres. Unperturbed, the mutated ant-men move in to the attack. Will you draw your sword to defend yourself (turn to **218**) or will you look for something else to use against the Xoroa (turn to **139**)?

264

The blast is just too much for the ages-old tunnel; the roof caves in on top of you and crushes the life out of your body.

265

The small round bottle is full of what appears to be swirling black smoke, giving it its colour. The glass stopper is sealed with hard-baked clay. If you ever want to break the seal and open the bottle, turn to **398** (make a note of this). Now, however, return to **339**.

266

You weaken under the priestess's relentless stare. Deduct 6 points from your STAMINA and 2 points from your SKILL. However, somehow you manage to keep moving and stagger towards the dais in order to attack the priestess. Seeing you approach, she breaks her concentration and you are released from the strength-sapping gaze. Turn to **350**.

267

The fireball misses your head by mere centimetres, exploding into a pillar. Before they can try anything else, you run at your reptilian attackers with your sword drawn; turn to **50**.

268

You slide to a stop close to a large web, which is made up of a tangle of shimmering, sticky, silver strands, in a high cavern. You scramble quickly to your feet as the web's maker descends from the roof of the cave. Facing you is a massive grey-black spider, almost five metres across. Instead of having the head of an arachnid, as you would expect, its hairy body is surmounted by a demonic head with a malevolent travesty of a human face, and wearing a Djaratian head-dress. As the diabolical creature stalks towards you, there is no doubt in your mind that your opponent is a Death Spider.

DEATH SPIDER   SKILL 12   STAMINA 9

The Death Spider will try to bite you when it attacks. If it wins an Attack Round, as well as losing 2 STAMINA points you must roll two dice. If the result is less than or equal to your POISON score, turn to 59. If it is greater, add 1 to your POISON total and continue your battle. If you win against this awesome adversary, turn to 120.

269

There are two ways in which you can fight the Mummies with fire. The first is to use a torch, if you have one, as a weapon. If you do this, turn to 325 and fight as normal; however, if you win an Attack Round, your weapon will inflict 4 STAMINA points of damage rather than the usual 2. (If you choose this course of action, you must also reduce your Attack Strength by 1 point because you are using an unfamiliar weapon.)

The second method involving fire is to throw a fire source – such as a lamp, a Yokka Egg or a burning skin of oil – at the corpse. Roll one dice and add 2: this is the number of undead you will have to get past. For each Mummy you attack in this way, *Test your Skill*; if you succeed, the Mummy perishes in flames. If you destroy all your opponents this way, you break through the Mummies' ranks and run to the shrines (turn to **295**) or the Temple of Sithera (turn to **395**). If you fail to stop all the Mummies this way, or if you run out of fire sources, turn to **325** but ignore the instruction there to roll dice.

270

You take the sandstone statuette from your backpack and show it to the Shaman. He explains that the deity it represents is Assamarra, the now almost forgotten God of the Sands. Return to **194**.

271

After a few vain attempts, you manage to secure the grapple over a rocky outcrop above the tunnel entrance opposite and, gripping the rope for dear life, you swing across the crevasse. Turn to **169**.

272

Suddenly there is a commotion in the water round you: you are being attacked by several vicious Snapper-fish. Roll one dice, add 6 and divide the total by 2 (rounding fractions up) to see how many you have to fight. Each Snapperfish has SKILL 6 and STAMINA 2, and the bite from such a creature does 3 points of damage to your STAMINA on a roll of 4–6 on one dice. If you survive your encounter, you go on. Roll one dice. If you roll 1–3, turn to **287**; if you roll 4–6, turn to **69**.

273

Desperately you sprint away through the boulders. *Test your Luck*. If you are Lucky, you escape safely; turn to **250**. If you are Unlucky, turn to **106**.

274

The surface of the gaming-table is divided into fifty squares and at either end is a row of counters; one set is black and one set white. The whole set-up looks like this:

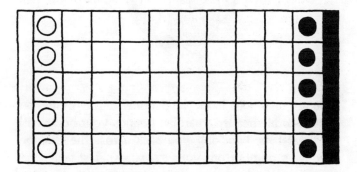

Nemset explains that the idea of the game is to get one of your pieces to the other end of the board; the first person to do so wins the game. Pieces can move one or two squares forward at a time but in no other direction. However, if, on your turn, your way is blocked by a piece directly in front of yours, you may move your piece just one square into an empty space on either side (but not backwards); this is the only time when you can move sideways. A good tactic is to try to trap your opponent's pieces so that they cannot move. Nemset chooses to play white and directs you where to move her pieces, while you are black. White goes first. *Test your Skill*, adding 2 to the dice roll. If you succeed, turn to **53**. If you fail, turn to **129**.

275

You are unable to harm the Sentinel of the Shrine, but the crocodile-headed guardian pounds your body with its great fists, knocking you back across the chamber (deduct 5 points from your STAMINA). *Test your Luck*. If you are Lucky, you manage to open the door and escape from the shrine (the Sentinel does not follow you once you are outside its chamber); turn to **284**. If you are Unlucky, the metal giant blocks your way out of the sanctum and exacts the punishment reserved for all thieves. Defenceless against its attacks, your adventure ends here.

276

You descend into the valley and cautiously creep towards the entrance of the tomb, trying to avoid the attentions of the lizards. *Test your Skill*, adding 2 to the dice roll. If you are successful, turn to **348**. If you fail, turn to **306**.

277

You scramble down the slope until you are standing in the sandy arena in front of the platform. The façade of the low building is decorated with the busts of people – or possibly of gods – standing in recessed alcoves.

'Who dares trespass in the Theatre of the Gods?'

The booming voice makes you jump almost out of your skin in surprise. The words echo around among the empty tiers of seats, but the voice itself seems to be coming from a dark doorway in the front of the building. What will you do now? Will you:

Answer, apologizing for trespassing?	Turn to **366**
Answer, demanding that the owner of the voice show himself?	Turn to **98**
Say nothing and approach the doorway?	Turn to **321**
Leave the Theatre of the Gods and continue your quest?	Turn to **8**

278

Will you now make your way to Sithera's forbidding temple (turn to **395**) or will you first explore the tombs of the Djaratians, if you have not already done so (turn to **149**)?

279

You miss your footing and slip. Automatically you reach out for something to hold on to, but the stone you grab is loose and comes away from the face of the pinnacle. There is nothing you can do to stop yourself falling. If you failed your first *Test Your Skill* roll, turn to **17**. If you failed the second, turn to **93**. If you failed the third, turn to **207**.

280

The sheer rock walls on either side of the river are covered with phosphorescent lichen, so you are able to assess your progress by its dim glow as you are carried downstream. You suddenly become aware of something moving towards you in the water ahead – then the Snapperfish attack. Although only a little larger than a man's hand, the Snapperfish is a savage carnivore with powerful jaws and needle-like teeth. The bite from one of these creatures does 3 points of damage to your STAMINA on a roll of 4–6 on one dice! Partially submerged in the fast-flowing river, you can fight these vicious predators one at a time, but with your Attack Strength reduced by 1 point.

	SKILL	SKILL
First SNAPPERFISH	6	2
Second SNAPPERFISH	6	2
Third SNAPPERFISH	6	3

If you kill all the fish, turn to **4**.

You are at the lower end of a long, vaulted passage which ascends steeply ahead of you. The walls of the Grand Gallery are carved with reliefs depicting a mighty king meeting the gods in the afterworld. At its top you enter a high-ceilinged chamber, on the far side of which is a great stone door, ornately carved and with a magnificent gold lock, flanked by two huge statues of a Djaratian king. The statues' expressions have been exquisitely fashioned, but their cold eyes and the cruel smiles turning the corners of their stern mouths bring a chill to your spine. This must be Akharis — even these carved images of him fill you with dread; it is as if the evil king knows that his return to power is imminent and considers your attempt to stop it to be futile.

Then you notice the blazing red eyes in the gloom of a corner of the anteroom. With a roar, a massive, shaggy-haired black beast leaps out of the shadows and paws the ground in front of you. The monstrous, dog-like creature snarls and bares its gleaming fangs. Facing you is the Guardian of the Dead of Djaratian myth, menacing protector of burial places and executioner of any trespassers who would desecrate the tombs of the kings.

GUARDIAN OF
  THE DEAD   SKILL 10   STAMINA 10

If you manage to overcome this mighty opponent, turn to 364.

282

Wiping the lizard's blood from your sword, you survey the cavern. On the far side you can see a mound of loose earth with a hollow in the top, in which rest two sandy-coloured eggs. Around the nest are scattered the bones of wild dogs and even pieces of a human skeleton. If you want to search the debris, turn to 65. Otherwise, you have no option but to leave the Rasaur's cave; turn to 226.

283

There is nothing lying on top of the column – but, as you are about to leave, you experience a weird sensation: your body feels warm and you become aware of a peculiar vibration, accompanied by a deep thrumming sound. The whole sensation is not unpleasant, and you almost feel as if you are being revitalized – and you are! This is the power of the magical geometry of the pyramid which allows the bodies of the dead to be preserved so well and for so long. However, you are not dead, so the effects of the pyramid's regenerative power are all the more beneficial. Roll one dice (if you have a Crystal Pyramid, add 1 to the number rolled). If you roll 1–2, turn to 327; 3–4, turn to 392; 5 or above, turn to 341.

284

The tunnel emerges in a square chamber which is painted with scenes of the dead king's journey through the underworld. In the wall opposite stands an ornate darkwood door; to the left and right, corridors lead elsewhere, the one to the left ending abruptly at another door. As you listen in the stillness of the tomb, a faint whispering sound comes from beyond the door in front of you. Where will you go now?

Through the door in front of you?   Turn to **177**
Through the door to the left?   Turn to **393**
Along the passage to the right?   Turn to **239**

285

The world solidifies round you again – but to your horror you see that you are still in the crumbling temple. Lopar does not have the power to teleport you from such a great distance away! You have saved Allansia from the Curse of Akharis but, as the temple falls in over you, your adventure, and your life, ends here, entombed in the Necropolis of the ancient Djaratian kings.

286

'You would need two hundred and eighty-six blocks of stone altogether,' you say. The ghost, obviously hearing you in ancient Djaratian, stops its muttering and looks directly at you. 'Of course,' the old man says slowly, 'that's right! Thank you, stranger. Tell me, who is it who has released me from my torment?' You tell the ghost your name, and in return he introduces himself as Rhehotep, the architect who designed and built the tomb, along with many of its death-traps. 'I was misled and ambitious. When the tomb was completed, I was buried alive in this room so that I could never reveal its secrets. I was working on that problem before I was killed, and I have been unable to rest ever since. Thanks to you, I may now depart to the Field of Reeds, where the sun never sets; but before I go, how may I help you in return?' Hurriedly you tell Rhehotep about your quest. You may question Rhehotep on two of the subjects listed below (you will be sent back to this paragraph after each choice). When you have made two choices, turn to **225** at once.

Guards and monsters in the tomb.	Turn to **101**
Traps you may encounter.	Turn to **27**
Charms you might need.	Turn to **133**
The Cult of the Cobra.	Turn to **334**
Akharis.	Turn to **365**

287

Totally lost, you wander dejectedly about in the water-filled corridors. *Test your Luck*. If you are Lucky, turn to **100**. If you are Unlucky, turn to **369**.

288

Which symbol will you press next, the scarab (turn to **141**) or the snake (turn to **104**)?

289

With one mighty wrench you snap the chains free from the pillars. Before the two cultists can react, you swing the chains at them and knock them both out! Then you grab your sword and backpack. Most of the cultists are still unaware of what is going on. Do you want to attack them (turn to **338**), or would you rather attack the Mummies in order to reach the High Priestess and stop the ritual (turn to **160**)?

290

With every muscle aching under the strain, you heave against the granite block of the sarcophagus – and it gives! A dark hole appears below the coffin and soon you have opened a gap big enough to squeeze through. You find yourself at the top of a flight of steps which disappear into the darkness below. You run down it as the sand starts to pour into the secret tunnel, and find yourself standing at the edge of a subterranean lake in a huge natural cavern. Phosphorescent moss is growing on its walls and stalactites hang down from the ceiling, many metres above you. Far off in the distance you can see a great wall, on the other side of which you can just make out the tops of ancient Djaratian buildings. Moored at the edge of the lake is a long, narrow boat. This is Akharis's funerary barque and your means of crossing the Sacred Lake. Unmooring the barque, you climb aboard and, taking an oar in your hands, guide the boat over the still waters. On the other side of the lake, you step out by a great gate, set into the wall above a flight of steps. The gate creaks open and you enter the grand entrance hall beyond. Torches round its walls immediately flare into life and you step back in surprise. Sitting in the centre of the hall is a gigantic creature with the body of a lioness but the head of a woman. Surely this is the legendary Sphinx! In a growling voice the Sphinx addresses you in ancient Djaratian. If you can understand it, you know what to do. If you don't, turn to **262**.

291

In the language of the Pygmy tribesmen of the jungles of southern Arantis, 'yokka' means 'sun'. According to their lore, Yokka Eggs are laid by the fabulously rare Yokka Birds: the birds fly down from the sun to lay their eggs on the cool earth and what hatches from these eggs resembles a ball of fire. You may throw an egg at an opponent at the start of a battle and, if you *Test your Skill* sucessfully, it will hit, break open and release the Yokka Bird, which will burn your enemy, causing damage to his STAMINA equal to one dice roll, before it flies away into the sky. Now return to **15**.

292

You take a run-up at the chasm and, when you reach its edge, you leap forward into the air. Roll two dice and add 6 to the total rolled. If the new total is less than or equal to your STAMINA, turn to **169**. If it is greater, turn to **332**.

293

Leaving your sword sheathed, you run at the Mummy in an attempt to remove the glittering death-mask. Fight the following combat in the usual manner but with your Attack Strength reduced by 3 points. Also, if you win an Attack Round you do not wound Akharis, you merely manage to avoid his blows; of course, if he wins an Attack Round, you suffer the usual damage.

AKHARIS   SKILL 13

If at any time your Attack Strength is 3 or more points greater than your opponent's, turn to **203**. You can give up this method of attack at any time and instead try to destroy the sarcophagus (turn to **257**) or simply resort to attacking Akharis with your sword (turn to **97**).

294

Climbing over the boulders, you peer over a rocky ledge and are startled by what you see. Lying entangled in a net, which has been staked down, is a huge creature, almost six metres in length; it has the body of an enormous lion and massive clawed feet. As it struggles to free itself from the net, you see that its large head is leonine but its teeth are more like those of a dragon. Its mane is golden, as is the rest of its sleek and powerful-looking body, and a pair of small, leathery wings sprout from its shoulder – a Dracon! The trapped beast has not noticed you yet, so will you leave here before it does (turn to **250**), remain in your hiding place and wait to see what happens (turn to **37**), or climb down between the boulders and approach the Dracon (turn to **174**)?

295

All the shrines have been either plundered or desecrated – except for one. Amid the destruction one, small, tomb-like structure has been left untouched. Nearing the building, you sense a strong aura of Goodness washing over you like a refreshing wave. What could be inside to create this atmosphere of calm? You could open the door of the tomb and enter it (turn to **317**) or leave here without further delay (turn to **278**).

296

After several minutes' walking, you come to a point where a side-passage comes in from the left to join the one you are following. Will you take this new tunnel (turn to **370**) or continue on your present route (turn to **130**)?

297

You gulp down the liquid and feel a surge of energy shoot through your body. (Restore STAMINA points up to half your *Initial* STAMINA score, rounding fractions up.) The viper's venom was like a Potion of Strength! Your muscles charged with new power, you flee the temple. Turn to **2**.

298

Between the towering cliffs you find yourself in cooling shade. However, you have not gone far along the gorge when you hear the sound of rock bouncing off rock, then an ominous rumbling noise. Looking up, you see, hurtling down at you from the cliffs, a boulder which in turn has started a landslide. *Test your Luck*. If you are Lucky, turn to **57**. If you are Unlucky, turn to **123**.

299

At last you have found it! In front of you, illuminated by your light, is Akharis's burial chamber and, in its exact centre, his great sealed stone sarcophagus. Excitedly, you run into the vaulted chamber. With a deep, resonating boom, a monolithic block of granite drops down from the roof of the tunnel, sealing off the only way out. Too late you realize what is wrong with the burial chamber: its walls are rough-hewn and undecorated, as is the sarcophagus. You heave the stone coffin open and, just as you feared, find it empty. This burial chamber is a fake: a trap to lure the unwary. There is no way out!

300

The heat is unbearable and, before you are half-way across the chamber, you lose consciousness. As the strength of the flames intensifies, your adventure comes to an end.

301

With each corridor looking much like the last, you soon become disorientated. At the next junction will you go:

Left, then right?	Turn to **383**
Right, then left?	Turn to **272**
Right, then right again?	Turn to **217**
Right, and then straight on?	Turn to **48**

302

At last the spell holding the swarm together in its wasp-form is broken by your spirited attack and the remaining insects disperse. As you pause for a moment to recover from your latest battle, you can see no sign of the cultist; however, you have the feeling that you will meet him again before your journey is done. Looking at Jerran's map, you calculate the general position of the tomb of Akharis and the distance you will have to travel to reach it. With renewed determination you set off in an easterly direction, away from the temple.

Eventually the sand-covered plain meets the barren hills to the east again and the way onward looks to be hard going. However, not far to the north-east the mouth of the valley opens on to the fringes of the Desert of Skulls itself. From Jerran's map it looks as if you could take this route to reach Akharis's tomb and, although it may take slightly longer, the going will probably be easier. Which route will you choose: the desert one (turn to **131**) or the path through the hills (turn to **62**)?

303

What will you use against the Mummies: your sword (turn to **325**) or fire (turn to **269**)?

304

Test your Luck. If you are Lucky, turn to **167**. If you are Unlucky, turn to **86**.

305

Everywhere you look, the hard granite walls of the tomb are covered in carved reliefs depicting the life of the evil Akharis. One particular stretch you pass shows slaves being put to death in front of a huge image of Sithera as a giant, four-armed woman with a snake's head. Absorbed in studying these ghastly carvings, you almost miss an archway to your right. Shining your light into it, you see a long, pillared hall. Do you want to enter it and explore further (turn to **30**) or will you keep walking along this passage (turn to **377**)?

306

The great beasts detect your movement and lumber into your path. The aggressive creatures attack instantly. You will have to defeat these huge reptiles before you can enter the tomb, since they are now blocking the way in to the entrance.

	SKILL	STAMINA
First GIANT LIZARD	8	9
Second GIANT LIZARD	8	8

If either of the lizards wins an Attack Round, roll one dice. On a 6, the beast hits you with its tail, which knocks you over as well as inflicting 2 points of damage to your STAMINA. It takes you one Attack Round to get up again, during which time the monster gets in an unopposed strike. If you win, turn to **33**.

Having lit your light, you make your way along the passage, able to see about ten metres ahead of you. The tunnel soon ends at the top of a steep flight of steps, cut out of the rock, that leads down into the darkness.

A tunnel leads onwards, but this one is faced with stone. Following this new passageway, you soon emerge in a long, pillared hall. You cannot see its end, and in the flickering light you can just make out the ceiling, high above you. Your light also picks out intricate Djaratian carvings covering the pillars and walls; they depict priests and servants carrying offerings, all looking towards the interior of the tomb. You pause in awe at the skill of the ancient Djaratians whose achievements have lasted for centuries. Suddenly the whole chamber is lit up in a burst of vermilion fire as a flaming ball flies past your head. In shocked surprise you face your attacker. Standing next to a pillar in the distance is a figure wearing voluminous robes of linen and muslin. In one scaly hand it holds a curved sword and you see that its head, far from being human, is that of a snake! In horror you realize that you are facing one of the Caarth, the legendary Snake People of the Desert of Skulls! The Caarth raises its free hand and another fireball forms in its palm as a second Snakeman, wielding a cruelly jagged blade, steps out from behind a pillar a few metres away. As the warrior advances towards you, the sorcerer releases the fireball. Work out Attack Strengths for both you and the Caarth sorcerer (who has a SKILL of 10) but do not deduct any STAMINA points. If your Attack Strength is higher, turn to **267**. If the sorcerer's Attack Strength is higher, turn to **335**. If they are the same, calculate them again.

308

Wielding the Sandworm's tooth, you must reduce your Attack Strength by 1 point as you engage the Golem in battle because you are used to using a sword. However, this unusual weapon will not make any difference against the insubstantial magical creature as it will pass straight through the Sand Golem's shifting form and so will cause it only 1 STAMINA point of damage (2 STAMINA points after a successful *Test for Luck*). However, hits from the magical creature are like punches from an iron gauntlet covered in sandpaper and will still inflict 2 STAMINA points of damage on you!

SAND GOLEM   SKILL 8   STAMINA 9

If you reduce your opponent's STAMINA to zero, you break the spell animating the Golem, and it becomes a harmless heap of sand once more (turn to **183**).

309

The priestess's relentless stare bores into you and you collapse at the foot of the dais. A smile forms on the woman's lips as you continue to weaken until you are totally drained of your life-force, which will be fed to Akharis's undead spirit to give him life once more.

310

Remembering the actor's words about the primitive inhabitants of these parts, you can well imagine that this gorge would make a perfect place from which to ambush unwary travellers. Will you carry on directly through the gorge regardless (turn to **298**), or will you detour to one side and climb up to the cliff-top in order to avoid the route between them (turn to **387**)?

311

You hang for a moment by your arms from the lip of the hole, then you let go. You fall at least ten metres before hitting the sand-covered floor of the chamber below (deduct 3 points from your STAMINA). If you are carrying any Yokka Eggs, *Test your Luck*, adding 2 to the dice roll. If you are Lucky, turn to **202**; if you are Unlucky, turn to **49**. If you do not have any Yokka Eggs, turn to **202**.

312

The sandstone statuette, half a metre tall, is of a regal-looking man, bare-chested and wearing a simple cloth round his waist. On his head is a tall, cylindrical crown with nine bands round it. In one hand he holds a long staff. Return to **339**.

313

The orb reveals no guidance and so, deciding you have no more time to lose, you flee from the temple. Turn to **2**.

314

Nothing untoward happens, so now will you press the scarab followed by the vulture (turn to **157**) or the vulture and then the scarab (turn to **104**)?

315

The door is unlocked and, pushing it open, you are almost blinded. You are standing at the entrance to a large room with marbled walls, and it is full of fabulous treasures. The countless gold and silver artefacts reflect the illumination shed by your light, making a quite dazzling display. Adjusting your eyes to this brilliance after the gloom of the endless tunnels, you gaze in awe at the goblets, statues, gilded chariots, royal furniture and caskets brimming with yet more wondrous items. You could spend some time searching this room for possible charms, or just for some choice treasure (turn to **359**), or you can leave and follow the passage back past the T-junction (turn to **105**).

316

Observing that you have killed two of its companions, the largest baboon screams in fury and hurls its boulder at you. *Test your Skill*. If you succeed, you dodge the missile. If you fail, the rock hits you a glancing blow and knocks you over (deduct 2 points from your STAMINA and reduce your Attack Strength by 2 for the first Attack Round in the ensuing battle). The Great Baboon bounds down the cliff to demonstrate to you what happens to anyone who strays into the territory of its tribe. Your blade still covered in the blood of its fellows, you engage the furious animal in combat.

GREAT BABOON   SKILL 8   STAMINA 7

If you win, the remaining baboons recognize your superiority in battle and escape up into the cliffs, hooting with fear. You are left to pass through the gorge unhindered, although you sense their eyes on you for as long as you are walking between the towering cliffs. Once you are through the gorge, the land levels out again and you head east. Turn to **90**.

317

You push the door open with ease and enter a lavishly furnished burial-chamber. The charms of Good protecting this tomb have saved it from the ravages of the evil ones. Lying on an ornate Djaratian couch is a body wrapped from head to toe in constricting bandages which have preserved it perfectly. As you approach, the Mummy does not move. You cannot help thinking that you may be able to gain further assistance here – but how? If you have some Oil of Lotus, turn to **384**. Otherwise, you will have to go out of this tomb, leaving everything in place (turn to **278**).

318

The floor immediately gives way beneath you and, with nothing to grab, you cannot stop yourself plunging into the spike-filled pit ... with fatal results. Your adventure comes to a gruesome end in the Tomb of Akharis.

319

The rocks out of the way at last, you can enter the passage. For as far as you can see there is nothing remarkable about it, certainly nothing to justify sealing it off. The passage soon comes to a dead end in a bare, small, square chamber. You suddenly become aware of a phosphorescence in the middle of the room and, as you watch, the ghostly figure of a short, middle-aged man, with an anxious expression on his face, materializes in front of you. He is dressed just like some of the people in the carvings on the walls of the tomb, and is mumbling something over and over to himself in a language you do not understand but which you presume to be ancient Djaratian. Unable to communicate with the ghost, you sense no aura of Evil round it — but nor do you detect any great presence of Goodness. The chamber is totally empty, so there is nothing left for you to do but leave the ghost to its mumblings. Turn to **154**.

320

'Mortal,' the Sphinx growls, 'all who would enter the Necropolis must first be judged worthy; therefore you must answer my three riddles correctly. If you should lie or prove ignorant, your punishment will indeed be terrible. But first, tell me, why do you seek to enter the City of the Dead?' In reply, will you tell the Sphinx all about your quest to stop Akharis (turn to **175**), or will you simply say that you are an adventurer exploring the ruins of the lost civilization (turn to **361**)?

321

A short figure suddenly appears in the doorway. The man is dressed in plain grey robes and is wearing a mask with grotesquely exaggerated features. 'No one trespasses in the Theatre of the Gods without facing the wrath of Cranno the Great!' he booms. Then, at a single word from the strange man, a huge Sabre-toothed Tiger bounds through the doorway and across the sand to attack you before you can reach its master.

SABRE-TOOTHED TIGER   SKILL 9   STAMINA 8

If you win, turn to **237**.

322

'Farewell, brave adventurer,' says the ghost. 'Remember, Akharis gains strength from his coffin.' As you leave her tomb, the spirit of Princess Nemset adds, 'May the gods of Djarat favour the noble-hearted.' Turn to **278**.

323

It is very well hidden, but eventually you do discover the hair-line crack that gives away the position of the door; not far from it, one section of carving is slightly more pronounced. Pressing your hand against it, the door creaks open and you enter a very small room. Resting on a slab are several objects of interest: one is a small, earthenware jar containing a mummified package; the second is a fabulous breastplate made from gold and lapis lazuli in the form of a falcon, each of its sixty feathers carefully fashioned; and the third is a tiny sarcophagus, only fifty centimetres long. You may take either or both the earthenware jar and the Falcon Breastplate – but then what will you do about the sarcophagus? Will you open it (turn to **381**), or would you rather leave it alone and be on your way (turn to **254**)?

324

The hole is actually the entrance to a natural tunnel. The air inside it is hot and dry. The tunnel does not go very far before opening into a small cavern. At this time of day the sun's rays penetrate even this subterranean chamber. Suddenly you hear the grating sound of scales on stone and the scratching of claws. You spin around, to see a large, reptilian creature with a long, dragon-like head and fang-filled mouth running at you from out of the shadows on six crocodile legs. A black tongue snakes out from between the Rasaur's jaws as it dashes towards you. You must fight this carnivorous reptile.

RASAUR   SKILL 8   STAMINA 9

If the Rasaur wins an Attack Round, roll one dice. On a roll of 4 to 6, it will hit you with its tongue, on the end of which is a poison gland (deduct 1 further STAMINA point and add 1 to your POISON score). If you win, turn to **282**.

325

The Mummies move forward stiffly to attack the one they believe has defiled their resting-places. Roll one dice and add 2 to the number rolled; this is the number of Mummies you must get past in order to reach freedom. Because they are so slow-moving, you can fight them one at a time. However, if any individual battle should last more than nine Attack Rounds, turn to **399** immediately. (Any Mummies you have already destroyed come from the top of the list.)

	SKILL	STAMINA
ANCIENT MUMMY	7	9
FESTERING MUMMY	8	8
DENU OF TEZRA	8	10
LORD SARROTH	9	12
ZOTH-LAR	9	11
CROWNED MUMMY	8	11
DECAYED MUMMY	7	10
PTAHNEM THE MIGHTY	10	12

If you should defeat all the Mummies, you make good your escape to the shrines (turn to **295**) or the black pyramid (turn to **395**) before they can come back to life!

326

The translation of the inscription on the wall above the map is as follows:

The dead king's body was carried from the City of Tezra thirty kilometres to the edge of the hills wherein lie the alabaster quarries. South of the Pillars of Antep the evil one rested for three days within the temple before being carried to his tomb. The infernal king ordered its construction decades before, and within its depths were countless traps and unspeakable horrors to ensure his eternal sleep was undisturbed.

Their duties finished, the priests and embalmers left the rift in the hills between the Gold Tunnels and the Oasis of Iash but only one returned alive, the rest having all suffered the Curse.

Now return to **346**.

327

You feel invigorated and ready to face any new challenges. Restore your STAMINA score to its *Initial* level, reduce your POISON score by 4 points and regain 1 LUCK point. Climbing down from the pillar, you leave the chamber; turn to **16**.

328

Sandworms' teeth, serrated along one edge, are fashioned into strong ivory daggers by the nomads of the Desert of Skulls and are prized possessions. Now return to **15**.

Plunging your hands into the petals, you send a cloud of pollen into the air and inhale a great lungful. Unfortunately the pollen of the Bloodfire Rose is highly poisonous; however, your increased immunity means that all you suffer is watering eyes and a violent wheezing fit which leaves you feeling drained – but it is better than death! Deduct 2 points from your STAMINA and add 3 to your POISON total. All you find as a result of your efforts is an earthenware pot, decorated with prayers for protection in the afterlife. Looking inside it, you find something wrapped in mummifying bandages and soaked in embalming fluids. You can think of no use for such an object but, if you want to take it with you, add it to your *Adventure Sheet*. Leaving the long-dead kings alone once more, will you try the other door out of the main chamber (turn to 177) or leave via the other corridor (turn to 239)?

330

You watch in satisfaction as the Mummy is consumed by fire. The flames rage for several seconds but then rapidly die down and go out. Horrified, you see that Akharis is totally unharmed! To prevent such a death, his Mummy has been protected with fire-warding spells and potions. As you stand, stupefied, Akharis lashes out with a mighty fist (deduct 2 points from your STAMINA). Turn to **215**.

331

You quickly put as much distance as possible between yourself and the mounds. Fortunately the remainder of your trek across the desert is without incident and eventually you find yourself heading back into the hills to search for Akharis's tomb. Turn to **62**.

332

The strength of your jump is not great enough to carry you to the other side of the crevasse. *Test your Luck*. If you are Lucky, turn to **386**. If you are Unlucky, turn to **353**.

You manage to make your way safely to the cave entrance at the base of the great boulder. After a few metres the rough-hewn tunnel opens out into a vast chamber in the centre of the massive boulder. A fire burns in the middle of the chamber, the smoke rising up through a hole in the roof. Sitting, cross-legged, on the far side of the fire is the figure of a man, his head bowed. 'Who seeks Lopar, the Shaman of Spirit Rock?' the man asks from the shadows. Sensing the man's aura of Goodness you announce yourself. 'And what is your purpose in seeking me?' he asks. Quickly you explain your quest to Lopar. When he looks up suddenly, by the flickering firelight you see that his head is that of a dog. Woven into his fur are various beads and feathers, and his hands resemble paws. 'Knowledge can be a dangerous thing in the hands of the ignorant,' the Shaman says sagely. 'Having braved Spirit Rock, you must prove that you are worthy to receive my wisdom by solving my riddle.' Startled, you listen to Lopar's conundrum:

> 'No army can stand against my might,
> I am greater than the wind or sea.
> All succumb just as day follows night.
> High mountains turn to dust before me.'

If you know the answer to the riddle, convert the letters of the answer into numbers using the code A = 1, B = 2, C = 3 . . . Z = 26. Add the numbers together, then turn to the paragraph whose number is the same as the total. If the paragraph makes no sense, or if you cannot solve the riddle, turn to **161**.

334

'The members of the vile cult are led by the High Priestess of Sithera, a devious and cunning woman possessed of dark powers and cruel magics. Avoid them if you can.' Return to **286**.

335

The sorcerer's magical attack slams into your body, surrounding you for a moment in vermilion fire (deduct 4 points from your STAMINA). In agony you prepare to defend yourself against these reptilian attackers; turn to **50**.

336

Against all the odds, you have done it – after countless centuries, Akharis is dead! Regain 1 LUCK point. All that remains is for you to burn his undead remains and then . . . A terrible groaning sound, coming from high above you, and gasps of terror from the cultists cause you to look up at the statue of Sithera. Just when you thought it was all over, the great statue's eyes are glowing with a sinister light and the colossus is coming creakily to life. The statue sweeps a taloned arm at you which you manage to dodge before it can hit you. Your non-magical weapon will have no effect on the animated statue, so what can you possibly use to defeat it? If you have an ankh among your possessions, you will know how many precious stones it has set into it. Multiply this number by twelve, then turn to the paragraph with the same number. If you do not have an ankh, turn to **73**.

337

Under Glantanka's unrelenting gaze you travel on through the heat of the day. The uneven path leads you further into the wilderness that fringes the Desert of Skulls. You follow the route north-westwards across boulder-strewn hills and through narrow valleys. As you pass through one rocky gulley you notice a large hole at its base, leading underground. Do you want to stop and investigate this entrance into the earth (turn to 324) or will you continue on your way without hesitation (turn to 226)?

338

Although you manage to cut down several of the cultists, you are hugely outnumbered, and the rest soon have you under restraint again. There is nothing you can do now as the High Priestess drains you of your life-energies, which she will use to resurrect her master, Akharis! Your adventure is over.

339

You give Cranno a brief outline of your mission without revealing too many important details. 'Indeed I may,' he says, removing the mask and revealing himself to be middle-aged, grey-haired and balding. He leads you through a doorway into the stone building; you find yourself in a long room, full of pieces of faded scenery and other theatrical props. 'You know, I used to be one of the greatest actors Allansia has ever seen,' Cranno says. 'I have played all the great parts: Duke Merion of Kallamehr, Quor the Sorcerer, Vorga the Pirate-lord. You understand I mean no harm really, what with the mask and dramatic performance. I just prefer to spend my retirement away from unappreciative audiences.' You are startled to see a huge Sabre-toothed Tiger pad over to the actor and lick his hand. 'Don't mind Cleomina,' Cranno adds. 'She's perfectly loyal. Anyway, about my aiding you. I've collected a number of interesting pieces; I would gladly swap some trinket you may possess for two of these items.' Cranno would like any one of the following: a Brass Telescope, a Healing Draught, some Oil of Lotus or a Crystal Pyramid. In return, you may choose two items from the list below if you decide to trade. Having chosen your items, turn to the paragraph relevant to each object to find out more about your new possessions.

Papyrus Scroll	Turn to **74**
Carved Bone Horn	Turn to **128**
Old Lamp	Turn to **354**
Statuette of a god	Turn to **312**
Large Bronze Key	Turn to **224**
Sealed Black Bottle	Turn to **265**

When you have finished here, you thank Cranno for his help and leave the ruined Theatre of the Gods (turn to **8**).

340

The cultist is busy doing something in front of the wall of the chamber next to the statue. Suddenly a section swings open and the man steps through into darkness. You run into the room but, before you can reach the secret door, it slams shut with a hollow boom. You try to force the slab of stone open again by pushing against it and using your sword as a lever, but all to no effect. There must be some hidden catch or lever that will open the secret door. Then you see it: on the front of the slab, surrounded by hieroglyphs, three symbols have been carved out of the wall on squares of stone that look as if they can be pressed inwards. The three symbols are a snake, a scarab beetle and a vulture. If you do not want to take the risk of trying to open this door, you follow the original tunnel, which turns to the right before coming to a flight of stone steps that take you deeper into the tomb (turn to **216**). If you do want to attempt to open the secret door, which symbol will you press first:

The snake?	Turn to **314**
The scarab?	Turn to **19**
The vulture?	Turn to **288**

341

The power of the pyramid converges on the spot where you are standing, filling you with new strength and relieving you of all stresses. Restore your STAMINA, SKILL and LUCK to their *Initial* scores, and reduce your POISON score to zero. Under the effect of the mystic energy, the blade of your sword actually sharpens, so that from now on you may add 1 to your Attack Strength in battle. With renewed determination you leave the chamber to continue your quest; turn to **16**.

342

'I, too, am on a quest of the utmost importance,' he says, grandly. 'I am Don Huan Fernandez, a knight of

Vastille, and this is my manservant, Gordo.' The tubby man nods and wipes the sweat from his forehead with a grimy handkerchief. 'I have sworn to rid these wild and desperate lands of the foul giants who dwell here, preying on the honest village-folk of this province,' he continues. 'Tell me, have you seen any such monsters in your wanderings?' When you shake your head Don Huan looks downcast and disappointed. 'Fear not. I am sure that my quest will soon be over and, with its completion, I shall win my lady's hand. Fare you well!' With that, the eccentric knight gallops off again towards the north-east, with the mule bearing his manservant trotting along behind, leaving you to continue your journey on foot. Turn to **24**.

343

You come to an abrupt halt against the sticky tangle of a gigantic web. You struggle to free yourself from the gelatinous strands but to no avail. Feeling as helpless as a trapped fly, you can do nothing when a shadowy black shape descends from the roof of the cave on to the web. The last thing you feel in this world is the demonic Death Spider sinking its fangs into your body.

344

The Evil Eye spell being cast by the High Priestess drains the energy from your muscles; in desperation you try to force yourself to keep moving and reach the woman. *Test your Luck*. If you are Lucky, turn to **266**. If you are Unlucky, turn to **309**.

345

As the Giant Scorpion twitches its last, you run over to help Jerran. He is barely alive. 'This is the end for me,' he gasps, 'but you must go on. Stop the Cult of the Cobra, and beware the Curse of Akharis.' With that, the brave archaeologist dies. The next morning you bury Jerran Farr, marking the grave with his old, battered hat. Offering a prayer to the gods for his departed soul, at the same time you swear to do all you can to stop the evil sect and prevent Akharis's return. Taking Jerran's map with you, you set off again, heading north.

By mid-morning your path is becoming gradually steeper as it leads you into the rocky foothills of the mountains which border the Desert of Skulls. You continue to follow the dusty trail as it turns towards the north-east. A few kilometres on, standing at the top of a ridge, you see that several semi-circular tiers of stone seats have been cut out of the base of the hillside in front of a raised platform and a low, rectangular stone building. Close to the seemingly deserted site lie fallen pillars and the remains of walls. Do you want to descend the hillside and investigate the ruins (turn to 277) or would you rather continue on your way (turn to 8)?

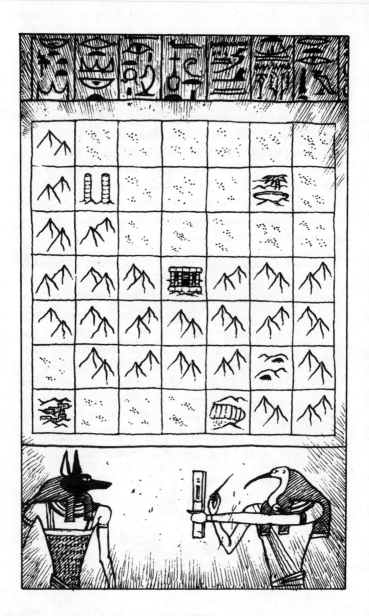

346

All that remains of the temple are sections of crumbling stone walls and the occasional colonnade of rounded pillars. Broken statues of strange, animal-headed deities protrude from heaps of drifted sand, while worn carvings adorn fallen stone slabs. An unnatural stillness pervades this place and the only sound you can hear is the desert wind keening through the ancient columns. Wandering among the ruins, you come to a part of the temple that is not in ruins. Entering the building, you discover that its interior is dimly lit by daylight streaming in through cracks in the roof. The walls of the temple are covered with stylized paintings of human and semi-human figures. A repeated theme appears to be that of a king praying, making offerings, or conversing with an assortment of gods and goddesses.

At last you come to a chamber in which, carved on one wall, is a map of the area round the temple at the edge of the Desert of Skulls; although it is recognizable as such, there are also several obvious differences. Pictures of buildings and other sites have been carved as part of the map and at the top of the wall there is a Djaratian inscription. You study the illustration to try to work out the location of Akharis's tomb. If you can, you will know how many kilometres it is to Akharis's tomb (turn to the paragraph with the same number to continue your adventure). Otherwise, your adventure ends here, as you have no idea where to start looking for the tomb. Soon you and many others will suffer the Curse of Akharis!

You find yourself in a long entrance hall. In front of you is a tall archway and on either side of it is a carved relief of Sithera, Goddess of Evil, ten metres high! Two cultists, their red robes bearing the motif of a rearing golden cobra, suddenly run through the archway, their curved swords drawn. As you prepare to fight, you feel something strike you in the back and the world goes black . . .

Slowly you come to and take in your predicament. You are chained between two great pillars, your arms stretched out on either side of your body. You have been captured by the Cult of the Cobra! You have no idea how long you have been unconscious, but you have recovered in time to witness the ritual that will end in Akharis's resurrection! You are being held prisoner at one end of a vast chamber inside the Temple of Sithera. At the other end is a huge, ten-metre tall statue of the snake-headed goddess, her four taloned arms raised menacingly. Beneath the statue, on a raised dais, lies a large stone sarcophagus inside which is the mummified body of Akharis! The Mummy is huge and wears an ornate death-mask which covers most of the dead king's rotting face. At the base of the dais stand two large braziers, the magical fires of which fill the chamber with an unearthly glow. Standing between the braziers is a strikingly beautiful woman with black hair cut in the style of the ancient Djaratians. She is dressed in the robes of a Djaratian priestess, and in one hand she holds a staff, the top of which is carved to resemble a cobra's head. She is chanting an incantation in ancient Djaratian, and it is repeated by the crowd of cultists who stand between you and the dais. You are also horrified to see that a mass of Mummies, in various states of decay, are blocking the way to the High Priestess. These must be the Mummies of those loyal to Akharis, returned to life by the evil cult. You must stop this ritual! Standing slightly in front of you, on either side, are two cultists who are totally caught up by the ceremony in front of you. One holds your sword and the other has your backpack. But how are you to get free? In desperation you drag at the chains and feel one give slightly. The chains must have been here for centuries and they have weakened over time. If only you are strong enough ... Roll three dice. If the total rolled is less than or equal to your STAMINA, turn to **289**. If it is greater, turn to **388**.

348

Before the lizards can react to your presence you have run past them and through the dark portal. Regain 1 LUCK point and turn to **204**.

349

Having been granted the Wisdom of Khunam, you understand perfectly what the ghost is saying. '... If the first level of the pyramid is made up of one block of stone, and the second level is made up of nine blocks, how many blocks would be needed to make a pyramid six levels high? If the first level ...' The ghost is repeating the problem over and over without ever arriving at the solution. If you know the answer, you could try calling it out (turn to the paragraph with the same number as the answer). If you do not know the solution, or if you do not want to waste any more time here, turn to **154**.

350

Swinging your sword, you try to strike the High Priestess and so prevent her using her evil curse-magic against you again. To defend herself, the woman raises her cobra staff, which suddenly twists in her hands and comes to life! If the Priestess wins an Attack Round and hits you with the staff, as well as deducting the usual 2 points from your STAMINA you must add 1 to your POISON total!

HIGH PRIESTESS   SKILL 9   STAMINA 7

If you win, turn to **397**.

351

You decide against exploring the Scarab's burrow as you will not find any Djaratian treasures up there; you would be more likely to find the beetle's mate or maggot-like young. Squeezing past the great insect's body and cleaning your sword of the thick yellow mess that clings to it, you make your way along the passage; this turns left again, before ending at yet another flight of stone steps. You descend them, even though they take you even deeper into the tomb. Turn to **216**.

352

Finding hand-holds in the crevices between the blocks of granite gives you no difficulty and, having climbed several metres, your light illuminates another corridor leading away from you. Do you want to pull yourself up out of the shaft to investigate this new passage (turn to **281**), or would you prefer to descend once more to the tunnel below and follow that (turn to **299**)?

353

Your jump misses the entrance to the tunnel and you smash into the rock-face below it. As you fall towards the river down the side of the crevasse, your head hits a projecting outcrop, which knocks you senseless. Unconscious in the fast-flowing river, you soon drown. Your adventure is over.

354

Rubbing the lamp fails to summon any supernatural spirits, but you do discover that there is still some oil left inside it. Return to **339**.

355

You unstopper the bottle and gulp down its contents. The water is cool and refreshing and has incredible revitalizing effects on you (restore STAMINA points equivalent to half your *Initial* score, 2 SKILL points and 2 LUCK points, and reduce your POISON total by half). Cross the Waters of Life off your *Adventure Sheet*, then return to the paragraph you just came from.

356

You walk up to the platform and inspect the ancient chest. Seeing no sign of any hidden traps, you carefully lift off its lid. You are surprised to discover that the chest is full of dried crimson flower petals, which could be hiding something. Do you want to rummage through the petals in case they are (turn to **329**), or will you leave this chamber and go through the other door (turn to **177**) or along the passage (turn to **239**)?

357

The stone hits you squarely on the side of the head. The blow leaves you dazed and with a painful bruise on your temple (deduct 2 points from your STAMINA and reduce your Attack Strength for the next battle you fight by 1 point). Meanwhile, the mutated ant-men move in to attack. Will you draw your sword to defend yourself (turn to **218**) or will you look for something else to use against the Xoroa (turn to **139**)?

358

You are sure that you can see an image forming in the centre of the orb: it is a figure with beads and feathers woven into its fur, and the dog-like face confirms that you have contacted Lopar, the Shaman of Spirit Rock! You call out to Lopar, and he looks in your direction. Somewhat surprised, he greets you and you hurriedly tell him of your success in your quest and of your present predicament. 'Then we must get you out straight away,' Lopar says anxiously. 'I will try to teleport you out – but I must warn you that you are a long distance away and I may not have the strength to lift and carry you over such a distance.' The Shaman's expression changes to one of deep concentration and the world round you grows hazy. *Test your Luck*. If you are Lucky, turn to **400**. If you are Unlucky, turn to **285**.

359

You cannot believe how many riches there are in this chamber. With half of what is here you could probably buy the whole of Rimon! It is only at the last moment that you hear your attacker's approach. Spinning around and drawing your sword in the same motion, you confront your would-be assailant.

Standing before you is a terrifying apparition: it is the corpse of an old man, clothed in scarlet and gold robes, but there is not a single drop of moisture left within it! Sunken eyes stare at you from a face dried tight over the man's skull. In places the desiccated skin has torn so that yellowed bone is visible, making the undead horror appear even more dreadful. Amentut was Akharis's Vizier, so loyal that the king demanded he be buried alive with his master, so that Amentut might serve him in the afterlife. One such duty is the protection of his lord's treasure-rooms – and you have been caught red-handed!

AMENTUT	SKILL 7	STAMINA 7

If the undead Vizier wins an Attack Round, roll one dice; if you roll a 6, Amentut clutches your skin and drains part of your life-force away. Deduct 1 point from both your *Initial* and current STAMINA scores and 1 point from both your *Initial* and current SKILL scores as you physically age! Amentut feeds on this life-force himself, so add 1 to his STAMINA score if he manages to do this. If you defeat the horror, turn to **221**.

360

As soon as Lopar sees the golden T-shaped cross, he gasps in amazement. 'My friend, you have here one of the most highly venerated and powerful artefacts of the ancient Djaratians. This is the Ankh, the Key of Life. Guard it well, for it may be precisely what you need to defeat the Cult and Akharis, should he return!' Now return to **194**.

361

'You lie!' the Sphinx roars and leaps at you. Your earthly weapon has no effect on this agent of the gods of Djarat. You are knocked flat by the beast, which then proceeds to tear you limb from limb so that you perish quickly, if horribly!

362

Test your Luck and *Test your Skill*. If you are both Lucky and successful, turn to **127**. Otherwise, you cannot stop the relentless descent of the spiked roof, and you suffer a horrible death in the Fangs of Sithera.

363

You manage to get to your feet before the cultists attack. Separated, Farr takes on one of the red-robed assassins, while the other two advance on you. You must fight them both at the same time.

	SKILL	STAMINA
First CULTIST	7	7
Second CULTIST	7	6

As soon as you have killed one of the cultists, turn to **214**.

364

The great beast slumps to the ground and breathes its last. You are sure that beyond the ornate door lies Akharis's burial chamber, but do you have a key to fit the golden lock? If you have, turn to the paragraph with the same number as that of the hieroglyphs inscribed on the key. If you haven't, no amount of force will make the great stone door budge, so at the last hurdle you have failed in your quest.

365

You ask Rhehotep how you may be able to destroy the mummified body of Akharis. 'Such undead are susceptible to fire,' the architect explains. 'It is also rumoured that his death-mask is imbued with life-giving energies. Destroy that, and you may destroy his earthly body.' Return to **286**.

366

A short figure appears in the open doorway, dressed in plain grey robes and wearing a mask with grotesquely exaggerated features. 'What do you want of the great Cranno?' the little man booms. Will you:

Ask if he can aid you in your quest?	Turn to **339**
Ask him what he knows of the Shaman?	Turn to **389**
Attack the man?	Turn to **134**
Leave the ruined theatre?	Turn to **8**

367

As the last Mummy falls, you find yourself at the foot of the raised dais — in front of you stands the High Priestess of the Cult of the Cobra! Most of the cult have been left confused by your attack and are running around in panic and chaos, but their leader remains cold and calculating. You have interrupted the Ritual of Resurrection and now must prepare to face the fury of Sithera's acolyte. Are you wearing a Malachite Amulet? If so, turn to **223**. If you aren't, turn to **121**.

368

The image of Cracca, Lord of Rivers and Ferryman of the Gods, falls at last and instantly changes back into a thirty-centimetre-tall statue. Now drained of its magical energies, the golden image is harmless and you may add it to your possessions if you wish. There is nothing else of value in the shrine, so you leave; turn to **284**.

369

Constantly wading through waist-high water while holding your light and sword aloft is very tiring (deduct 1 point from your STAMINA). The tunnel veers sharply to the left and then left again. At the next junction, will you go left (turn to **383**), right (turn to **195**) or keep straight on (turn to **142**)?

370

Not far down the tunnel, you discover that the roof has caved in, blocking it completely and smashing a hole through the floor of the passage into a chamber below. What will you do now? If you have a rope and grapple, you could lower a light down through the hole (turn to **385**) or climb down the rope yourself into the chamber (turn to **202**). If you do not have a rope, you could risk lowering yourself through the hole (turn to **311**). Alternatively, you can retrace your steps and turn either left, if you have not already done so (turn to **130**), or right (turn to **63**)?

371

The corridor gradually slopes upwards until, ducking under a low archway, you emerge in a high, pyramidal chamber, its four walls coming together at a point several metres above you. In the wall opposite is the entrance to another tunnel, but in the centre of the room a few steps go up to the top of a small, squat pillar. Do you want to climb the steps to the top of the pillar (turn to **283**) or would you rather leave this chamber (turn to **16**)?

372

Scrambling over the rocks, you come upon an open space in the boulder-strewn wilderness. Lying on the ground on his back is Don Huan Fernandez and standing over him is a grotesque, three-metre-tall humanoid. Its lumpy skin is coloured a sandy brown and it is naked except for a loincloth made of animal hides. In one huge hand it carries a great wooden club embedded with chunks of flint, but it is its face that fills you with dread. The monstrosity has just one large eye in the centre of its forehead and an ugly horn sprouting from the top of its skull. Fernandez is fending off the Cyclops with what remains of his shattered lance. Lying close by is the motionless body of Fernandez's steed, while you can see his cowardly manservant hiding in a crevice in the rocks. You do not give much for the old knight's chances of surviving this battle. Will you:

Draw your sword and run to his defence?	Turn to **248**
Try to distract the Cyclops?	Turn to **181**
Leave Fernandez to his fate?	Turn to **114**

373

The sarcophagus shatters in an explosion of stone shards. Some of the lumps of rock hit you (lose 3 STAMINA points) but Akharis comes off worse. The sarcophagus was what partly restored the Mummy's strength, but you have robbed him of those life-giving energies; reduce his STAMINA score by 6 points when you come to fight the weakened Akharis. However, your adversary is now almost upon you. Will you attack him with the Waters of Life, if you have them (turn to **64**), or with your sword (turn to **97**), or will you try to remove his death-mask (turn to **293**).

374

As you make your way along the tunnel, you become aware that the temperature of the air in the tomb is rising rapidly until you begin to feel uncomfortably hot. After descending a short flight of roughly cut steps, the corridor curves to the right and now is lit by an orange glow, so that you no longer need your light to see by. As you turn the corner you have to shield your face from the light and heat! Ahead of you the passage enters a square chamber, where it becomes a bridge over a fiery pit. Roaring flames leap up on either side of the path and you see everything through a heat-haze. However, this is the only way ahead, so you must brave the Path of Flames. Walking across the stone bridge, you begin to feel dizzy as the heat intensifies. Roll three dice. If the total rolled is less than or equal to your STAMINA score, turn to **115**. If it is greater, turn to **300**.

375

A low growling awakens you in the middle of the night, and in seconds you are on your feet, your sword drawn. With a snarl two jackals, attracted by the light of your fire, leap at you. Fight them together.

	SKILL	STAMINA
First JACKAL	6	5
Second JACKAL	5	5

If you defeat the animals, you manage to get a few more precious hours of sleep before dawn, when you set off to the north for the temple. Turn to **5**.

376

Pushing with all your strength against its lid, you open the sarcophagus — only to discover that Akharis's mummified body is not here! However, his guardian spirit or 'Ka' is. Like a glittering silhouette of a man, with no distinct features, the Ka sits up in the otherwise empty stone coffin and reaches for you, determined to acquire your life-force for Akharis.

KA   SKILL 8   STAMINA 7

Despite its insubstantial form, the Ka can still be injured by your weapon. If you defeat the guardian spirit, turn to **252**.

377

The floor of the tunnel begins to slope gradually downwards, while the ceiling remains at the same height. There are no steps and the tunnel is getting steeper, the loose sand covering the stone floor making it treacherously slippery underfoot. Suddenly you lose your footing and tumble, head over heels, down the slope. *Test your Luck*. If you are Unlucky, turn to **343**. If you are Lucky, turn to **268**.

378

Brandishing the statuette in front of the Golem has no effect, but can you invoke its power? If you know the name of the deity whose image you hold in your hand, convert the letters of the name into numbers using the code A = 1, B = 2, C = 3 ... Z = 26. Add the numbers together then turn to the paragraph whose number is the same as the total. If you do not know the god's name, you have no choice but to draw your sword, since the Golem is upon you (turn to **143**).

379

Abandoning the peculiar potions, you make your way towards the exit from these chambers. Turning a corner, you find your way blocked by three bizarre creatures: a jackal, a tiger and a cobra, but they have been mummified. If you want to attack the bestial guardians with your sword, turn to **163**. If you would prefer to use fire, turn to **25**.

380

As Nandibears regularly remove treasure from their homes, having no need of it themselves, all you manage to find are a few Gold Pieces lying among the carcasses (roll one dice to see how many). Finding nothing else of value, you leave the monster's lair and rejoin the trail heading north-westwards towards the temple. Turn to **337**.

381

Inside the sarcophagus is the partially bandaged, mummified body of a monkey. Its eyes suddenly flick open and, screeching, it leaps out of the sarcophagus at you, biting your arm (deduct 2 points from your STAMINA). Quickly you draw your sword and try to fend off the agile creature.

MUMMIFIED MONKEY SKILL 6 STAMINA 4

If you win, looking inside the sarcophagus again you find a large golden key, its head inscribed with thirty-four hieroglyphs that spell out the royal names of Akharis. Taking the key, and any other items you fancy, you leave the hidden room; turn to **254**.

382

'How disrespectful!' the creature snarls angrily. 'You humans have no manners at all. Clearly I shall have to teach you a lesson.' With a tremendous heave, the Dracon drags the stakes out of the ground and frees itself from the net. Roaring, the monster stalks towards you, ready to slash you with its huge claws and bite you with its oversized teeth.

DRACON SKILL 9 STAMINA 14

The Dracon derides your skill and mocks you as you engage in combat; as a result, you must reduce your Attack Strength by 1 point for the duration of this battle. If you reduce the creature's STAMINA to 5 points or less, turn at once to **61**.

383

You eventually find yourself back at the steps where you entered the flooded maze! After all your efforts you have not got anywhere (lose 1 LUCK point.) Turning back towards the maze, will you now go to the left (turn to **124**), to the right (turn to **234**) or keep going straight ahead (turn to **217**)?

384

Some intuitive feeling tells you to anoint the Mummy with the oil. As soon as you do so, a shimmering light appears next to the couch and forms into the glowing, blue-white figure of a Djaratian woman wearing fine clothes and a falcon-shaped head-dress. Then the ghostly lady speaks to you in dulcet tones: 'Stranger, why do you wake me from my sleep of eternity?' You feel compelled to be truthful, so you relate your mission to her. 'I am Princess Nemset, daughter of Horari, twenty-fourth king of Djarat,' the ghost says, 'and I will help you in your task to destroy the Evil One. But first, I long to play my favourite game, Tenet, again.' Nemset points to a table whose surface is divided into a grid and with playing pieces set up on it. 'If I teach you the rules, will you play against me?' the Princess asks sweetly.

Will you grant her request (turn to **274**) or, fearing that time is running short, will you tell her that you must leave at once (turn to **322**)?

385

Your light illuminates part of a large, rubble-strewn chamber, the sand-covered floor of which is at least ten metres below you. You will be able to climb down your rope safely into the chamber, if you wish (turn to **202**). If you do not want to, you must retrace your steps back to the original tunnel and turn either left, if you have not already done so (turn to **130**), or right (turn to **63**).

386

You hit the water with a tremendous splash and, momentarily stunned by its chill, are carried along by the fast-flowing underground river. Turn to **280**.

387

You half walk and half climb towards the cliff-tops. In a few places you slip, sending a cascade of stones down into the gorge, but eventually you reach the top safely. You must now eat a meal or lose 2 STAMINA points. Looking down at the landscape from your lofty vantage-point, you can see clearly as far as the edge of the hills to the Desert of Skulls and as far south as the Bay of Elkor. If you have a Brass Telescope and wish to use it, turn to **256**. Otherwise, turn to **235**.

388

You strain against the chains but your arduous adventure has exhausted you too much for you to be able to break them. The ritual reaches its climax and the High Priestess turns to face you. 'And now, Lord Akharis, Destroyer of Cities and Favoured of Sithera,' the High Priestess intones, 'take this mortal's life-energies and live again!' Your adventure ends here.

389

'The Shaman of the Wilderlands has his abode at Spirit Rock, a league to the east. But be warned, the lands beyond here are home to all manner of primitive and inhuman tribes.' You thank Cranno for his information (make a note of Cranno's Warning on your *Adventure Sheet*). Now will you ask him whether he can aid you on your quest (turn to **339**), or will you leave the theatre without further delay (turn to **8**)?

390

Wedging the paper package in the middle of the blockage, you light the fuse then run for cover towards the turning in the passageway. Before you can even reach it, the Firepowder explodes with a deafening boom. Dust showers down from cracks in the ceiling and the walls shudder under the force of the explosion. *Test your Luck.* If you are Lucky, turn to **319**. If you are Unlucky, turn to **264**.

391

Choosing a route up the side of Spirit Rock which seems to offer you the greatest number of hand- and foot-holds, you climb towards the cave entrance, fifty metres above you. *Test your Skill* three times. If you are successful every time, turn to **333**. If you fail any of the rolls, turn at once to **279**.

392

Restore both your STAMINA and SKILL to their *Initial* scores, and regain 2 LUCK points. You can also reduce your POISON total by 8 points. Feeling refreshed and rejuvenated, you leave the room along the new corridor; turn to **16**.

393

You enter a long room which is lined on both sides with the statutes of Djaratian kings. At the end of the room is a raised platform on which rests an ornate gilded chest, its lid adorned with falcon heads at each corner. You can see nothing else. If you want to take a closer look at the chest, turn to **356**. Otherwise, you leave the chamber and are faced with the choice of going through the other door (turn to **177**) or along the new passageway (turn to **239**).

394

You and Farr chase along the back street after the cultist but lose him among the hustle and bustle of an animal market. Then you catch sight of a red-robed figure, on the opposite side of the square, moving away from you. As you elbow your way through the crowd, you see a trader's cage swing open and, with a roar, its occupant leaps into the crowd. As the throng of people vanishes, you and Farr find yourselves alone in the middle of the square, facing the newly escaped Black Lion. Angry at having been locked up in a confined space and confused by its unnatural surroundings, the beast strikes Farr with one great paw, knocking him to the ground. You have no choice now but to try to stop the enraged animal.

BLACK LION   SKILL 9   STAMINA 9

If you win, turn to **28**.

395
Before you stands the forbidding black pyramid that is the Temple of Sithera! Your quarry and your fate lie within. At the foot of the pyramid, an avenue of pillars leads up to a large, dark opening, in front of which you can see two guards dressed in Djaratian garb. Will you boldly walk up to the entrance (turn to **132**) or look for another way into the temple (turn to **208**)?

396
You cannot have gone more than twenty metres along the passage when you feel a slab shift under your foot as you take your next step. *Test your Luck*. If you are Lucky, turn to **201**. If you are Unlucky, turn to **318**.

397

The High Priestess of the Cult of the Cobra falls to the dais with a dying cry: 'Oh Sithera, aid us now!' Then she breathes no more. You have succeeded in preventing the Priestess from completing the Ritual of Resurrection (regain 1 LUCK point)! Hearing angry shouts, you turn to see the now reorganized cultists advancing towards you. While you are wondering how you are going to get out of this situation alive, the cult suddenly stop, their attention focused on the dais behind you. With a lump in your throat, you turn to see that the eyes of the great statue of the goddess are glowing with a sinister light. A bandaged hand then rises above the lip of the stone coffin and grips the edge, followed by another, and the decomposing body of Akharis rises from the sarcophagus. The Mummy stands, almost two metres tall, and the long-dead Djaratian king pierces you with a look of pure hatred! Akharis's evil goddess must have intervened and used her dark powers from the Demonic Plane to complete the resurrection of her loyal servant. You must stop this horror or Akharis's curse will still be fulfilled. The Mummy moans balefully and lumbers stiffly towards you. You are going to have to act quickly to destroy Akharis. Will you:

Use fire against the Mummy?	Turn to 330
Use the Waters of Life (if you have them)?	Turn to 64
Try to use some earthenware jars (if you have any)?	Turn to 118
Use some other charm?	Turn to 85

Try to remove Akharis's death-mask?   Turn to **293**
Try to destroy the sarcophagus from
    which he was raised?   Turn to **257**
Attack the Mummy with your
    sword?   Turn to **97**

398

Having broken the seal, you unstopper the bottle. Immediately the swirling black smoke flows out of the bottle and forms into a vaguely humanoid-shaped cloud. You are just aware of a pair of darkly glinting eyes before the malevolent Nanka envelops you completely and flows back into the bottle, taking you with it! Your adventure ends here.

399

As you fight, the other undead surround you, their bandaged fists pounding into your body relentlessly until you can put up no further resistance. Your adventure is over.

400

With a final, terrible, thundering roar, the Temple of Sithera crashes to the ground – but you have already gone ... The world solidifies round you again, and you find yourself in the familiar surroundings of Lopar's cave inside Spirit Rock. The Shaman looks drained after casting the teleportation spell that brought you here, but you can also sense his relief. You are suddenly overcome by exhaustion, now that you are able to relax properly for the first time in days.

Eventually Lopar speaks: 'Your bravery, skill and quick wits have foiled Akharis's return to power and, for that, hundreds of unknowing people owe you a debt that can never be paid. But now you must rest. Lie down beside the fire and sleep.' And sleep you do, secure in the knowledge that you have thwarted the nefarious plans of the Cult of the Cobra and saved all Allansia from the Curse of the Mummy.

More Fighting Fantasy by Wizard Books

The Warlock of Firetop Mountain
Steve Jackson and Ian Livingstone

Deep in the caverns beneath Firetop Mountain lies an untold wealth of treasure, guarded by a powerful Warlock – or so the rumour goes. Several adventurers like yourself have set off for Firetop Mountain in search of the Warlock's hoard. None has ever returned. Do you dare follow them?

Your quest is to find the Warlock's treasure, hidden deep within a dungeon populated with a multitude of terrifying monsters. You will need courage, determination and a fair amount of luck if you are to survive all the traps and battles, and reach your goal – the innermost chambers of the Warlock's domain.

1 84046 387 2

The Citadel of Chaos
Steve Jackson

Deep inside the Citadel of Chaos, the dread sorcerer Balthus Dire is plotting the downfall of the goodfolk of the Vale of Willow. His battle plans are laid, his awesome army equipped, and attack is surely imminent.

Summoned by a desperate plea for help, YOU are the Vale of Willow's only hope. As star pupil of the Grand Wizard of Yore and a master sorcerer yourself, you must strike at the very heart of Balthus Dire's nightmare world. Though you command many powerful spells, the quest may be deadly, for who knows what creatures lie in wait in the Citadel of Chaos?

1 84046 389 9

Deathtrap Dungeon
Ian Livingstone

Down in the dark twisting labyrinth of Fang, unknown horrors await you. Devised by the devilish mind of Baron Sukumvit, the labyrinth is riddled with fiendish traps and bloodthirsty monsters, which will test your skills almost beyond the limit of endurance.

Countless adventurers before you have taken up the challenge of the Trial of Champions and walked through the carved mouth of the labyrinth, never to be seen again. Should you come out of the labyrinth alive, you will be wealthy beyond your dreams. Do YOU dare enter?

1 84046 388 0

Creature of Havoc
Steve Jackson

Evil is festering in Trolltooth Pass. The necromancer Zharradan Marr is close to stealing the secrets of Elven magic which would make him invincible. Nothing could then prevent his legions of Chaos from taking over the whole of Allansia ...

But what do you know or care about all this? In this unique adventure, YOU are the Creature of Havoc, a monstrous beast with a taste for fighting. Ruled only by hunger and rage, you have no knowledge of your past or destiny. If you survive, you may begin to control your bestial nature and learn your true purpose, but success is by no means certain, for the traps and terrors of Trolltooth Pass are many ...

1 84046 391 0

City of Thieves
Ian Livingstone

Terror stalks the night as Zanbar Bone and his bloodthirsty Moon Dogs hold the prosperous town of Silverton to ransom. YOU are an adventurer, a sword for hire, and the merchants of Silverton turn to you in their hour of need.

Your mission takes you along the dark, twisting streets of Port Blacksand to seek the help of the wizard Nicodemus. But Blacksand is riddled with thieves, assassins and foul creatures. Should you survive, you must journey to the most terrible place of all – the tower stronghold of the Night Prince himself, Zanbar Bone!

1 84046 397 X

Crypt of the Sorcerer
Ian Livingstone

An ancient evil is stirring in the bowels of the earth, and the land is blighted. After being entombed for one hundred years, the necromancer Razaak has been re-awoken and is poised to fulfil his promise of death and tyranny. His army of undead are at large across Allansia bringing death and destruction to all who resist.

It is up to YOU to find the only weapon to which Razaak is vulnerable – his own magic sword! Only then might you survive the dangers that await you in his evil lair – the Crypt of the Sorcerer!

1 84046 396 1

House of Hell
Steve Jackson

Stranded miles from anywhere on a dark and stormy night, your only hope of refuge is the strange, ramshackle mansion you can see in the distance …

But entering the House of Hell hurls you into an adventure of spine-chilling and blood-curdling terror. The dangers of the torrential storm outside are nothing compared to the nightmarish creatures that await you within its gruesome walls.

Be warned! You must try to keep your fear under control – collect too many FEAR points and you will die of fright. Can you make it through the night without being scared – to death?

1 84046 417 8

Sorcery! 1: The Shamutanti Hills
Steve Jackson

Based on the best-selling Fighting Fantasy gamebook system, *The Shamutanti Hills* is Book One in Steve Jackson's *Sorcery!* series. Your epic quest will take you across the mysterious hills to the cityport of Kharé, but only if you outwit the creatures, traps and wizardry you encounter along the way.

Play as either a warrior or as a wizard. If you choose wizardry, your survival will depend on your knowledge of the *Sorcery! Spell Book*'s darkest secrets. With many other unique features to discover, *Sorcery!* is a true challenge for novice and veteran adventurers alike.

1 84046 430 5

Eye of the Dragon
Ian Livingstone

In a tavern in Fang, a mysterious stranger offers YOU the chance to find the Golden Dragon, perhaps the most valuable treasure in all of Allansia. But it is hidden in a labyrinth beneath Darkwood Forest and is guarded by the most violent creatures and deadly traps.

To begin your quest YOU must drink a life-threatening potion, and to succeed you must find maps, clues, artefacts, magic items, jewels and an imprisoned dwarf.

1 84046 642 1

Talisman of Death
Steve Jackson and Ian Livingstone

The once-peaceful world of Orb is in terrible danger. Dark forces are at work to unleash the awesome might of the Evil One – and only YOU can stop them.

YOUR mission is to destroy the Talisman of Death before the Dark Lord's minions reach you. But beware! Time is running out…

1 84046 566 2

Sword of the Samurai
Steve Jackson and Ian Livingstone

The land of Hachiman is in grave danger. The Shogun's control is slipping. Bandits roam the land freely and barbarian invaders have begun to raid across the borders. All this because the Dai-Katana – the great sword Singing Death – has been stolen from the Shogun.

YOU are the Shogun's champion, a young Samurai. Your mission is to recover this wondrous sword from Ikiru, the Master of Shadows, who holds it hidden deep in the Pit of Demons.

1 84046 732 0

Bloodbones
Steve Jackson and Ian Livingstone

Bloodbones Lives!

The dreaded pirate-lord Cinnabar, scourge of the twelve seas, plagued the seafarers of the Old World in a bloody reign of terror until a brave adventurer put an end to his evil. But now he is back from the dead, seeking revenge, with the dark powers of voodoo at his command.

YOU have your own score to settle – Cinnabar murdered your family when you were a child. Only YOU can end the horrific slaughter by destroying the pirate captain and his crew of cut-throats. Come hell or high water Bloodbones must be stopped!

1 84046 765 7

The Official Fighting Fantasy Website

www.fightingfantasy.com

Visit the website for...

- Latest news on FF gamebooks and events
- The Adventurers' Guild, the official Fighting Fantasy Club!
- Competitions, Monster Gallery and gamebook maps
- Download screensavers, wallpaper, bookmarks and much more ...
- Exclusive information on all forthcoming FF gamebooks, including previews of cover art